to Rockey

COOL FOOL

Blues Rockin' In The Hammer

Doug Carter

COOL FOOL

Blues Rockin' In The Hammer

DOUG CARTER

Seraphim Editions

Library and Archives Canada Cataloguing in Publication

Carter, Doug, 1943-
Cool fool : blues rockin' in the Hammer / Doug Carter.

ISBN 978-0-9808879-8-3

1. Carter, Doug, 1943-. 2. Blues musicians--Canada--Biography.
3. Double bassists--Canada--Biography. 4. Blues (Music)--Ontario--
Hamilton--History. I. Title.

ML418.C323A3 2010   782.421643'092   C2010-902839-2

Cover Illustration: Doug Carter
Design: Kerry J. Schooley
Editing: Kerry J. Schooley
All pictures: Doug Carter except as noted in acknowledgements or as source unknown.

Published in 2010 by
Seraphim Editions,
54 Bay Street
Woodstock ON
Canada N4S 3K9

Printed and bound in Canada

Acknowledgements

Kerry Schooley for getting the ball rolling to turn the blog I'd started, *Cool Fool: Blues Rockin' In the Hammer* into a book and for his sense of beat style that he was able to infuse my words with and his considerable expertise and knowledge of how a book should work and how it should look.

Russell Carter for sharing with me his memories and photos (pg. 18, 19, 24, 46, 48,) of the early days playing Blues and Soul in Hamilton with his bands "The Bishops" and "The Master Hand."

Patti Stirling for the opportunity and space to actually put the book together and for her photos from the 1980s and 1990s (pg. 148, 149, 153, 159, 166, 168).

Julie Boden (pg. 133), Gary Deans (pg. 36), Brian Edwardson (pg. 56, 57), Sue Freestone (pg. 13, 16,) and Lynn MacIntyre (pg. 155, 156), for sharing their memories and photos.

Don't Bother Knockin'...this town is rockin', Patti Meyer, Gary Lee and Buffalo Sounds Press for the inside skinny on just what is the Buffalo Shuffle and the heads up on the connection between musicians from Hamilton and Buffalo going back to the late 1950s.

jam.canoe.ca for it's great encyclopaedia of Canadian musicians and bands and Wikipedia for being a useful and accessible depository of information about all things interesting.

All the cats and kittens I played with along the way. Without you there is no memoir.

Contents

Doin' The Buffalo Shuffle   1

Somethin's Got A Hold On Me   9

Goin' Down To William Street   27

Best Damn Blues Band In The World!   37

England Bound   55

Walkin' By Myself (After England)   75

Gotta Be A Good'un   95

Hot Times At The Hotel Tonight   113

Doin' The Snake   137

If The Boogie Woogie Kills Me I Don't Mind Dyin'
(All I Wanna Hear Are Those Downhome Blues)   161

Forword and Forward

This is my story, my memories, from my very subjective point of view. I've tried to capture the enthusiasm of the era, a golden age of pop music, and its roots in the Blues. I apologize if I've left anyone out that should have been included and I've done the best I can to confirm the spelling of the names I have used, but since 1959 was 60 years ago, etc., and memory being what it is, what you're holding, if not the truth exactly, is how I remember it.

I made very little money from my musical endeavours, if you don't count the $15 or so I get each year from the royalties for "Deaf, Dumb, Crippled & Blind" and "Caledonia River," two tunes I co-wrote with Richard Newell that, believe it or not, someone somewhere still gets out of the vaults to spin on air.

The women in all the lives I touch on in this memoir have been left out on purpose. That's another, and in some situations very complex, subject. I think I'll leave that for the soap opera version. In retrospect, the music ruled. As J.B. Lenoir wrote " ... the voodoo music has got the whole world in its spell." It sure as hell had me.

It's hard to express the appreciation I have for all the help everyone along the way gave me pursuing my dream. Having gone straight from high school to the cold mill at Dofasco, as it was once known, I knew early that the get-a-regular-day-job-with-a-pension-and-stick-to it-until-you're-65 was never going to work for me. Face the Burlington Street bus to Beach Road to & fro 5 days a week or hit the road and take a chance on life in a Rock'n'Roll band? Well, the next 150+ pages or so is my answer to that question.

Doin' The Buffalo Shuffle!

Live At the Bon Ton*, Buffalo, New York, 1964*
Were we excited?
Hell Yes!
Were we scared?

Shitless, looking out at that audience obviously wondering what the hell a bunch of white kids from Canada thought they were up to - blowin' the Blues - on stage -

WITH MUDDY WATERS!

Last thing I expected of that evening in the fall of 1964 was to find myself with buddies Richard Newell, Paul Cronkwright and Ronnie Copple on stage in front of a black audience at The Bon Ton, *the* Jazz and Blues club on the Niagara Frontier, or possibly in all of up-state New York, maybe the top Blues club anywhere along the shores of Lakes Erie and Ontario combined, but definitely the place to be where it counted most: East Ferrie and Waverly Streets, the black heart of downtown Buffalo, where people lived and loved the Blues every day of their eye-popping, ass-shaking, jive-motherfucking lives.

Scared?

For a moment the only rhythm in the room was the noise of our knees knocking, our only accompaniment, expectation:

> *low expectation*
> *the whole damned room holding its breath*
> *and then Richard started singing & blowing harp*
> *& we fell into the groove behind Muddy's drummer*
> *S. P. Leary*

because our drummer was back home with a not-tonight-honey headache or on a can't-get-out-of-it night shift pumping gas or maybe just pulling his dip-stick while unknowingly

beginning a lifetime of lying abed wondering where he'd been the night the rest of us, The Chessmen-less-one, a hard-driving, blue-eyed Blues band from Hamilton Ontario Canada, got to play for the first time on-stage with an official Chicago Blues drummer,

> *& did he know what to do!*
> *Shake my nerves & rattle my brain*

And there sitting, watching, off to one side of the stage was the great Muddy Waters HIMSELF, elegant, wearing a sharp, shiny, shark-skin, grey suit, matching shirt and tie like he'd just stepped out of the city's finest haberdashery. And a brand new, fresh DO. (To quote J. B. Lenoir: "don't you touch my head 'cause I just got a fresh process" = "DO" for which the do-rag is an essential element to hold it all together while everything sets—the process was done at the local barbershop. It de-kinked kinky hair and it built it up into a magnificent pompadour like the male version of a woman's beehive)

Richard Newell with Muddy Waters at the Bon Ton Club, Buffalo, NY, 1964.

> *& a black beauty queen on Muddy's natty arm.*

2

Our hero—our idol—the singer and band leader and slide guitar master on dozens of records stored in closets and on shelves in our bedrooms back home. The #1 Mississippi, electric Bluesman—watching—US!

How had the world come to this?

Dig: Richard Newell sitting in his funky little kitchen on East 25th Street, the middle of Hamilton Mountain, not really a mountain even, just a bend in the long curve of the Niagara Escarpment from up-state New York, winding through South Ontario before petering out under the waters of Lake Huron,
> & Rich is listening to WINE
> WINE in BUFFALO
> AM radio that runs down at sundown
> & "The Hound"
> George Lorenze
> HOWWWWOOOOOOOOOOOOO
> announces
> an upcoming engagement by Muddy Waters at the Bon Ton
> the very next weekend.

At last an opportunity to see Muddy live and on his turf in a black American neighbourhood, in front of people who had bought his records for years and made them R&B hits before white kids had been told "to go make that noise" in the garage or the basement or anywhere away from here. Before Elvis shook a hip. When it was the real shit, played in a way that left no doubt what that "Hound Dog" had been sniffin' aroun' after.

Sure, we'd seen Muddy and his band before. The previous year: 1963.
> At the First Floor Club
> in Toronto
> "The Good"
> Ontario

During the reign of The Lord's Day Act, the whole damn Province locked up on Sundays tighter than a parson's pucker, no booze allowed to interfere with religious observance and the Holy Day beginning at the tick of twelve o'clock Saturday night.

And The First Floor Club, bless them, essentially a coffee-house featuring acoustic folk music…*"and isn't the Blues, really, when you come right down to it, the folk music of our African American neighbours to the south?"*

Which is to say a roomful of white folks smiling politely with their hands clasped on table tops being confronted with a genuine, electrified, Chicago-style Blues band.

· DEC · 64

James Cotton wails.

Chicago! The Windy City! The City of Broad Shoulders, thick steaks and thicker pizzas and Jazz bars and south-side Blues bands who, finding themselves in uptight Toronto, played reserved, tenuous versions of songs that should have rocked out, should have screamed at those white folkies to get up and let their backbones slip. Okay, enjoyable and exciting for dedicated fans (hell, we couldn't believe Muddy had even showed up in Toronto) but still leaving us craving the real thing in it's own element.

By the time the weekend came 'round Richard had organized wheels and with a few other guys, yours truly included, shuffled off to Buffalo.

The Bon Ton had been a jumpin', with-it place for Jazz and R&B since back in the '50s. The club was on Woodlawn Avenue in the city's black district: Heading through the door we right-away realized we were the only white people in the club—

BUT WHO CARES?
there was Muddy Waters up in the far corner of the club &

NO COVER- JUST BUY BEER &
there was Muddy's band up on the
bandstand getting ready to play the first
set &

MAN WHAT A SET
—everything we could have hoped for:
the soon-to-be-legendary piano player,
Otis Spann, rollin' up the keyboard
in his trademark style, his left hand
holding down the shuffle boogie
beat and his right hand sprinkling
showers of high notes in answer to
the guitars, James Cotton riffin' on
his harp, Muddy sashaying his slide
guitar along with those mighty vocals
(man what a powerful voice he had;
strong enough to cut through the

Cotton talks to the
band. From left: S.P. Leary, Pee Wee
Madison, Milton Rector, Otis Spann

noise of a raucous room with a piss-ant sound system) and James "Pee Wee" Madison on guitar, Milton Rector on bass and the aforementioned S. P. Leary knockin' out that Chicago-outta'-Mississippi shuffle beat.

In the course of a typical night for the best portion of each set Muddy sits out, moving about the packed room, chatting at tables, mingling with the club's patrons while on stage the vocals are handled alternately between Otis Spann and James Cotton. Then for the conclusion of each long set Muddy joins the band on stage for steaming readings of his repertoire staples.

This was the real thing, the Blues where and as they should and have been played, but all fresh to us white Canuck kids back then. End of the first set and our pianist, Paul Cronkwright was either so pissed or so full of piss he went over to where the band was sitting and talked Muddy into letting Richard play part of the next set. Man, what was he thinking?

What WAS Muddy thinking? Maybe *here's some fun to break up the evening…send these, wise-ass kids back to Canada with their tails between their legs.* Before we knew it we were up there fingering our instruments, looking at a sea of black faces looking back at us with *The hell?* written on each and every one.

> *& then we were off -*
> *Richard led us through a mini-set of our best non-Muddy tunes, like*
> *Lonesome Sundown's "Gonna Stick To Ya' Baby" and*
> *Billy Boy Arnold's "Wish You Would"*
> *& when we finished the audience applauded.*

In particular they applauded that harmonica playing white kid from Canada who could

Cotton, Milton Rector and Otis Spann.

sing real good too. Actually the applause was thunderous, and appreciative, especially after Rich had sung and played harp. The thrill of our young lifetimes!

When James Cotton came back on stage he was all business now and maybe a little jealous of the attention Rich had received. Out came the classics.

> *first some Little Walter stuff:*
> *"Juke"*
> *"Off The Wall"*
> *and then into Sonny Boy Williamson II's:*
> *"Fattenin' Frogs For Snakes" &*
> *"Don't Start Me To Talkin' "*

—blowin' his ass off like we hadn't heard him do earlier in the evening, using classic tricks like sticking the harp in his mouth sideways and using his nose to blow through the reeds. Cotton sure improved his playing for the rest of that evening, taking it to another level. Even though Richard only blew a few tunes, it was enough to impress James Cotton. At the end of the night the experienced

Blues man told Rich that he was going to remember him. Over the years they met again several times and sure enough Cotton did remember the harmonica playing white kid from the Bon Ton.

We stayed to watch through the last set. How could we do anything else? Otis and James each sang a couple of tunes, Otis to our shock getting off the piano to do a James Brown imitation compete with slide/shuffle dancin' and splits and a whole bunch of that James Brown shtick, though I don't remember him doing the feeling-faint-and-throwing-a-cloak-over-his-shoulders bit. Then Muddy came back playing his hits.

And finally, THE FINALE. The highlight of a night that set the crowd to howling: Muddy singing "Mannish Boy". He started with his back to the audience, hardly moving, a slight sway to the shoulders, a little swing to the hips.

> *m-m-m-m-m-m-m-m-MAN*
> *he's playing with us, and something else*
> *m-m-m-m-m-m-m-m-MAN*
> *he turns around*
> *m-m-m-m-m-m-m-m-MAN*
> *there's a bulge at the front of his trousers*
> *m-m-m-m-m-m-m-m-MAN*
> *a significant bulge*
> *m-m-m-m-m-m-m-m-MAYAN*
> *at the back of the room they stand up on their chairs to see,*
> *m-m-m-m-m-m-m-m-MAYAN*
> *climb up on the tables even*
> *m-m-m-m-m-m-m-m-MAYAN*
> *Muddy playing with this thing in his "pocket"*
> *MAYAYAYAYAN*
> *thrusting his pelvis at the audience*
> *MAN*
> *Did I previously call Muddy elegant?*

spell M…
& did I mention the audience was can't-get-enough screamin' out loud?
…A…
I know I was sittin' there open-mouthed, dumb-struck, and what-the-fuck?
…N…
he reached way in his pocket & brought out a long-neck beer bottle
holding it up for the audience to see
MAN

Muddy shows the audience it was only a bottle down his pants.

The song done, they go straight to their theme, Jimmy Smith's "Back At The Chicken Shack" and the audience is out of its hand-smackin', mouth-whistlin', foot-stompin', motherlovin', collective mind. We're on our feet, The Chessmen, the audience, not wanting it to end, ever. When the dust settled people come over to shake our hands, wish us well. Muddy won't remember that night but I always will. Always.

What a feeling
"Son"
What a rush.
"Sweet Home Chicago"

All that encouragement, from the audience, from the band and from Muddy himself, had us believing, man, that we really could. Little old us, a bunch of white kids from nowhere Canada, not just could but would blow good, authentic Blues.

Amen.

Something's Got A Hold On Me

1959, hanging out at the Mountain Park at the north end of what's now Upper Gage, hovering from the escarpment over Gage Park and the city below. From here you could see practically everything in the east half of The Hammer, and as far as Toronto if there'd been anything to see in Toronto. Across Concession Street was Walt's Soda Bar, home of the most awesome looking Wurlitzer jukebox on Hamilton Mountain. It lit up with gurgley light running side to side across the top. It contained—wait for it—fifty

The Mountain Park Pavilion still stands today at Concession Street and Upper Gage. The building formerly housing Walt's Soda Bar is across the road in the background.

78 rpm records: one play, one nickel. Places like Walt's were tucked into neighbourhoods all over the city. They'd catered to the guys and gals a little older than us who got hip to Rock'n'Roll all the way back in '54, the year that rocked the world.

We'd heard the music—it was cool—but for us the most awesome thing about Walt's was the bank of early-generation pinball machines, again a nickel a play. Lost a lot of money in that joint. Still, something already had a hold on me. It started with Conway Twitty showing up at the Mountain Theatre further west on Concession Street by Upper Wentworth. It's only make believe isn't it? I mean, it must have been. 1957 and on Hamilton Mountain where nothing ever happened who could believe the Concession Street flicker-palace was packed to the doors with teenagers for a real 'live' Rock'n'Roll show? With RockaBilly un-sensation Harold Jenkins soon to be world famous as Conway Twitty. And Twitty rocked. Turned out he was playing the Flamingo Lounge downtown and somebody had booked him a matinee.

He always stayed at the Fisher Hotel, corner of Bay Street North and York Blvd. where local legend has it he wrote his #1 pop hit, "It's Only Make Believe," launching his Country music career. But even before all that, Twitty recommended Ronnie Hawkins try the Ontario bar circuit and then Sun Record label-mate Ray Smith too. They all came and they were all hits in The Hammer, Toronto and throughout Ontario. You can look it up in your history books. I wasn't inside for Conway's concert. Oh, but it sounded so good from the alley behind the theatre, the back doors open wide for this early fall concert.

Quick as a mutt in rut it was 1958 and Jerry Lee Lewis was at the Dundas Arena headlining a small Rock'n'Roll revue. His "High School Confidential" had just been released and was getting good airplay locally. We'd all loved Jerry from the first barrel roll of "Whole Lotta' Shakin' Goin' On." And there we were, Rich, me and some of the other guys from our gang.
Yeah—
gang
The Zactos
faded blue denim jean-jackets
chrome studs all over &
the skull & crossbones
in black on each shoulder.
See me comin', better step aside (Tennessee Ernie Ford "16 Tons")

I'd first met Richard Newell in 1957, same Grade 8 class at G.L. Armstrong School on

Concession Street at East 18th. Richard's parents were from England. They'd been dance hall operators in East London where the Family Newell was thick on the ground. More about that later. When Rich and his folks first came to Hamilton they had a fish 'n'chip shop at Brucedale and Upper Wentworth. By the time I met Rich, his father was a technician at Westinghouse working in radio or spy technology or one of those secret somethings that went on at the Longwood Road plant back in those days. We just sort of gravitated together. Similar interests like—

Rock'n'Roll (I guess!) &
drawing cartoons
etc.

But I gotta say that, from the get-go Richard had an, um, active sense of humour. He loved practical jokes, constantly delivering great one-liners and snarky put downs. We wasted hours browsing a King William Street joke shop where someone claims Rich palmed his first harmonica. Don't know about that but in our early Chessmen days a bunch of us were hanging outside The Downstairs, a favourite downtown after-hours blues club, waiting for the music to start. Richard got impatient waiting. He and Paul Cronkwright took off somewhere saying they'd see us in a while. Ten minutes or so drag by and suddenly there's a commotion across the street at The Flamingo Lounge. Richard and Paul come flying out the door followed by maybe everyone in the club, a few of whom chase Richard and Paul down the street. Paul had found some stink bombs somewhere and they'd snuck in and set a couple off in the washroom. Stunk the place out. Man people were pissed. The chase was on, up and down McNab Street, the boys hiding under parked cars. Didn't work. They were dragged out by their shit-kicking cuban heels and given a good thrashing.

I learned early on, hanging out at Mountain Park, that any time spent with Richard was not going to be dull. I'd already gotten into Rock'n'Roll in a big way the previous Xmas when my aunt gave me her old 78 rpm record player (plug it into any old radio with matching jack-holes on the back tell *me* the whole world wasn't randy) and some wax from the recent hit parade. Stuff like Elvis Presley's "Hound Dog," b/w "Don't Be Cruel," Bill Haley's world-wide smash, "Rock Around The Clock" & Jim Lowe's "Green Door," funky in a rockin' novelty way.

COOL FOOL

Getting ready for the dance: Doug and friend George Cooper in hair curlers

But I was pretty disappointed by Pat Boone's suck-the-life-out-of-it-version of Little Richard's "Tutti Frutti." I'd much rather have gotten the real thing. Same with a bunch of other top-ten type hits: Guy Mitchell's "Singin' The Blues" instead of Hank Ballard and The Midnighters' sexy "Work With Me Annie" or "Little Darlin' by The Diamonds instead of Clyde McPhatter and The Drifters' legendary you-can-get-anything-you-want-down-at "Three Thirty Three." But hey! No regrets, with our #1 RockaBilly hero in town at the Dundas Arena, Jerry Lee Lewis in a shiny, deep-wine coloured jacket that I lusted after. White pants and white boots; the man could dress. We were down in the front row and could hardly believe it. "Great Balls of Fire," "Breathless." "High School Confidential." And then—

Come a long a baby…
we shoved our way to the front of the stage,
Ow! Man. I burnt my arm on the footlights,
JERRY LEE! JERRY LEE! JERRY LEE!
Shake it baby shake it—
yell, cheer,
jump up & down,
"Whole Lotta' Shakin' Goin' On."

Midway through Jerry jumps up, back-kicks the piano stool across the stage and proceeds to wail away at the keys standing up. But he still isn't done. His leg comes up and he starts pounding the keyboard with his white boot!
We went wild!

Jerry Lee was the finale of a touring show that also featured Country singer Bobby Helms, (hit ballad "My Special Angel" and best known for the perpetual Xmas rocker "Jingle Bell

Rock") and the Casual Teens (doo-wop rocker "So
Tough"). We just knew we had to do that:
> learn to play &
> get up on stage &
> rock baby rock

A sensation confirmed. In 1959 when Buddy Knox of
"Party Doll" fame and Jimmy Bowen who'd had a minor
hit with "I'm Stickin' With You" and the Rhythm Orchids,
RockaBillies out of the American south-west, packed the
house at the Tivoli Theatre on James Street North, I knew.
> Yes
> by then I knew.
> I wanted to do that!
> I had to do that!

Attendance at these gigs was fuelled by record releases.
These days it's about downloading tunes and storing them in
some kind of memory but for us collecting began mainly with
7", 45 rpm vinyl. The ones with the big holes in the middle.
> No downloads
> No CD's
> No cassettes
> No 8-track

Striking a pose at the YWCA Dance

Seventy-eight rpm records were 10" and easily
breakable. Thirty three and one third long playing albums
had just been invented and not much of the music we
liked was available in that format. And of course you
couldn't play 33 1/3 "albums" "LPs" unless you updated your equipment (same as it ever is)
but 45s were very portable; you could carry a whole night's entertainment on your thumb

and most people had record players that would play them as well as the old-school 78s so everybody went to parties carrying their favourite discs. We'd tumble downstairs to the old basement rec-rooms, take command of the record player and run some black R&B, volume up as loud as it would go *hey baby do you want to dance?* Couple of good fast tunes then slip on one of those get-close-as-you-can slow numbers to create your own crotch-a-matic moments. Until you got slapped in the face slow down honey you're movin' way too fast; those were the days. I remember slow songs at high school dances and teachers walking around with rulers to measure the space between partners. 12 inches was required but it might as well have been miles, er, kilometers.

14

Twelve inches of you-know-what would have been useful back then.

All this measuring was to counteract the Dirty Boogie. Don't ask where it came from. It was just in the air. One of the first urban legend dance steps, the drift being that if you knew how to do it, well, it drew the girls like candy. It could be a little or—hold on—maybe a lot sex-u-al, depending on your partner. It seems to have originated out of Memphis, Tennessee and a Roscoe Gordon cut called "The Chicken" recorded at Sun Records and released originally on the Flip label and later as Sun Record 237.

> *work with me on it…come on & do the chicken with me*
> *ahhh, you got it baby*
> *now we're doin' the Dirty Boogie*
> *Say, where IS that teacher with the ruler?*

Dances sprang up all around Hamilton in the late '50s. Everybody was looking for places to shake their things. We learned the steps by watching each other or by tuning in to ABC TV's live-out-of-Philadelphia American Bandstand via Channel 7 in Buffalo which in those pre-cable/satellite days, in The Hammer anyway, you had to have a special antenna on your aerial stack to receive. The Philly show went national with host/DJ Dick Clark in 1957, but Buffalo didn't have an ABC affiliate until '58. But when it arrived, it meant one-and-a-half solid hours of Rock'n'Roll every afternoon starting at 3:30 pm. Those Philly kids wore the latest gear and were hip to the latest dance crazes. It was mostly dancing to hit records but once every half-hour you got to see a recording artist that might turn out to be someone you really liked covering their latest hit. Actually not playing live but lip-syncing to their own recordings. But who knew from that shit back then? Amazingly, in July 1961 the King Bee himself, Bluesman Slim Harpo, appeared on Bandstand! Jerry Lee Lewis was a Bandstand regular too until Clark fired him because Jerry had married his own 13 year-old cousin.

> *Tell me the whole world*
> *wasn't horny back then!*

Bandstand style TV dance party shows soon sprang up everywhere and somewhere in that time period Hamilton's own CHCH TV began Channel 11 Dance Party at its King Street

Sue Freestone and George Cooper groovin'.

West almost at Locke Street, studio hosted by the dashingly responsible Bill Lawrence. By the mid-60s, if you wanted your moves to groove on-screen, you had to boogie by co-host and camera magnet, Hamilton's very own Carol Ann Tidy, "Miss Dominion of Canada." Lawrence also chucked chins on the kiddie Tiny Talent Time revue before moving on to read the weather in Toronto, leaving Dance Party hipsters to the crazed machinations of Dave Mickie.

We watched the shows and then practiced our moves at local weekend dances held in public schools and community centres and church gymnasiums all around the city. Each dance featured a local DJ spinning a mix of personal favourites and hits from the CKOC or CHUM weekly record charts. A favourite DJ I recall grooving to was Norman B out in some Westdale church hall, where Jimmy Reed and other Blues discs by cats like Bobby "Blue" Bland were spun.

One of the best dances featuring live music was "The Alex," the Alexandra Roller Rink, on James Street South at Bold. There you could see local bands such as Nicky Moore and The Scepters, Cal-Jay and The Vermonts and The Five Pieces of Eight along with charted out of town recording artists like Bobby Curtola and the Arkansas RockaBilly sensation, Ronnie Hawkins with his (original) Hawks including Levon Helm on drums.

The local talent was good too.
> My gal is red hot
> you're gal ain't doodly squat

Jack Carter, vocalist (no relation) and Russ McAllister, guitar, both from The Vermonts, went on to start and front their own bands, having local success well into the '80s.

The bar scene in The Hammer was alive with rockin' action. The Grange on the south side of King Street West between James and McNab, The Flamingo Lounge around the corner on McNab South. Duffy's Tavern downstairs on the north side of King between John and Hughson where the Papalia mob sat at the very back of the club in a special white leather banquette and the Golden Rail a block east at John and King. Further afield were the Jockey Club (Ottawa and Barton), the Fisher Hotel (York at Bay) and Hanrahan's (Barton and West). Public watering holes on the city's Mountain were non-existent, the city hilltop dry as a bone. Getting a cold brew and maybe good rockin' or C&W entertainment meant exceeding the city limits south into Hannon and The Old Plantation House which was a stone cold Country joint. Later, when the newly-built Mohawk College filled the Mountain with thirsty students, Mundy's Family Restaurant became The Jamesway Tavern, on Upper James between Limeridge and Stone Church Roads. The Hillcrest at Concession St. and Upper Wentworth briefly became a supper club with middle of the road entertainment. I remember sneaking in and seeing a version of The Platters there. That was it for the longest time.

Not that it mattered to us. When we hung out the drinking age was twenty-one in bluenose Ontario. Depending on the joint, sneaking into most bars to see the music acts was tough for a mid-teen even with borrowed ID, making New York border-towns, where 18 was legal, the hot drinking spots. Puritan Ontario also restricted bars to open just 6 nights a week. Bar bands had Sundays off and would book one-nighters at Sunday night dances, especially if they could find a place en route between bar gigs. These Sunday dances sprung up in small towns all over Ontario. Thus, summer Sunday nights at Port Dover's Summer Gardens featured some awesome talent from the Ontario club circuit. A half-hour scoot south on Hwy. 6 to flash some style past the cottage talent, then beach-blanket out on Lake Erie sands hoping to steal third base in time to

The Flamingo, McNab Street South, Hamilton.
- source unknown

catch your ride back home.
Sure, I'll phone you baby.
What's that?
Your old man works at Stelco next to mine?
Aww, my girlfriend is gonna kill me!

If you were too young to drive (and drink) or couldn't get Pop's car for the Dover trip,

Saturday and Sunday night community-hall dances were the places to find new music acts. Most booked bands out of the Toronto area. Grab a bus and head down Barton Street to St. Nick's Church just east of Kenilworth. Or stop in at another long-lived venue, the Mount Hamilton YM-YWCA. Occasionally too, there were dances featuring name bands at the Polish Hall on Parkdale Ave. and The Chandelier Club on Barton St. E.

And, in 1961, at The Serbian Hall on Barton Street just east of Kenilworth Street, Ronnie Hawkins first introduced Robbie Robertson to local fans as his lead guitar. Everyone followed the Hawks back then. Rock'n'Roll band numero uno. Rumours had been swirling for weeks about Ronnie's awesome new guitarist and every fan and band member that didn't have a gig that night showed up to see if this new King of the Telecaster was as hot as the rumours said he was. I shouldn't have to tell you that he was. Soon Ronnie and his new Hawks, Robbie, Richard Manuel, Rick Danko and Levon Helm added Garth Hudson and filled the Alexandra Roller Rink, a barn of a place on James South. They blew us away, especially with their great rendition of Muddy Waters' "She's Only Nineteen Years Old."

Teen Age Night Club comes to Burlington.

In between the dance halls and the bars was The Downstairs club, coffeehouse by day, dance club by night. It was located on the south-east corner of McNab Street and King

West, entrance around the corner from The Grange, which was the "A" room in town and on the major Ontario bar circuit. Across McNab Street was The Flamingo Lounge, a "B" or maybe even "C+" room, a rough and rowdy joint that featured cats like Ray Smith, a Sun Records RockaBilly guy who followed Ronnie Hawkins into Southern Ontario and like Hawkins eventually settled in the area. Once again, Ontario's blue-laws defined the action, forcing bars to close at 11:30 Saturday nights. After midnight Saturdays, groups that played the right sort of music slid around from the licensed bars to play the unlicensed Downstairs club, turning the "coffeehouse" into Hamilton's basic, all night, Blues and R&B joint.

Ah! The Downstairs! Actually downstairs. Amen brother! Righteous marble steps. Iron railings painted turquoise blue. Stairs twist at bottom left to right. Through wallpaper walls. But look close at that wallpaper. Great, groovy, outta' sight, Folkways Records album-cover wallpaper!
I want it! I want it!

Now turn right through a door past the ticket taker and you have to buy a one-time membership and then pay an entrance fee. Or, if you're a known musician or a friend of the Shermans (Club operators and music impresarios) or have paid your annual dues or buy your suits regular at Jerry's Man's Shop (also owned by the Shermans) which most of the city's bands and hipsters who can afford suits do, why then you get in free.

Find yourself in a little red room. 8' x 8'. Dig the red leather coming halfway up the walls. Plush. Elegant. Wooooooo! A wall payphone. And a cigarette machine that rarely works but takes your money anyway. Hey, talk to Jerry eh! To your left a

Teentown Hardtimes Dance, Dundas Townhall 1960
From the left: Russell Carter, Nelson Flowers,
Bobby Washington, Reggie Washington, Billy Morris

"cloak room" used mostly for bands to relax, change and "refresh" themselves. A drink or two maybe between sets. Keep that bottle in the brown bag, man, this joint ain't licensed.

And there it is.
Straight ahead.
Waiting.
The main room.
THE CLUB!

Zoom. Slide inside the door—lookout for that. Listen to it ROAR. From the crowd. Can't you tell they're wowed? By the band? Hell no! BY THEMSELVES!

The main room is littered with square tables covered by standard, after hours, beatnik club, red and white checked tablecloths probably pinched from the laundry of a local Italian restaurant. The Stage: nothing but a large wooden platform supporting a beat-out, upright piano. (One night, the Chessmen gigging there, Richard ripped the entire keyboard out pretending to play like Jerry Lee Lewis. But that's another story.) Hanging on the walls are fake Victorian gas lamps and in between, painted in Hamilton, original, modern art. The ceiling of this joint is all pipes.

Water pipes.
Heating pipes.
Peace pipes.
Pipes, pipes, pipes.
Painted black.

The men's room is inhuman. Every time. Year after year. *Best find an alley to take your piss. Or wear an oxygen mask! No dumping unless you are absolutely already shit faced.* But you didn't come here to whiz. In the south-east corner next to the Men's is the kitchen, home of some weird 50-cent-a-glass cola that tastes, year in year out, like banana popsicles. But you can also get a vanilla coke: pop laced with flavouring extract anyone can pick up at almost any grocery store even though it contains an amazing amount of alcohol. The Club's corned beef on rye is mighty good too if it is late and you've drunk enough vanilla coke.

But the Bands, man, the bands! Jay and The Majestics, Billy and Lily and The Thunderbirds, John and Lee and The Checkmates, the list goes on and on, with local R&B faves The Bishops as house band. And Sunday afternoons the place hosts concerts featuring the likes of John Lee Hooker, Brownie McGhee and Sonny Terry, visitors to Hamilton several times over, plus Jazz acts like Toronto's Peter Appleyard. For a kid like me, familiar with a rocking, electrified, powerfully backed John Lee Hooker through his Vee Jay Records album *I'm John Lee Hooker*, seeing him with just a basic guitar wired into a small amp and sittin' by himself on a wooden stool was a major surprise—

What? Where's the band?
but wait, what a boogie-rama treat.
I said
BOOGIE-RAMA!

And never mind the rounders sittin' around waitin' to pound somebody out should they (you) get out of hand! Too a pulp! Gulp!
BOOGIE-RAMA!

Rock'n'Roll came to power in 1954 and peaked in 1959. The roll call of hits and songs that remained popular for decades is staggering still. And then it was over.

The powers that be decided the music needed toning down and sold the kids the "The Bobby's" and soft-Elvis and then the Brill Building stuff and along with them the girl groups and Philadelphia doo-wop and Phil Spector and on and on. Fortunately around the same time Detroit's Barry Gordy Jr., in the process of starting his own Motown record label, charted hits by Jackie Wilson and Marv Johnson and especially Barrett Strong's "Money." Ray Charles' 1959 groove-changing smash "What'd I Say" helped give birth to the Motown sound, keeping R&B alive until The Beatles and the The Rolling Stones and the rest of the British invasion could give it a fresh feel and sell it all back to us again.

What had hold of us first, me, Richard, Ronnie and the rest of the gang hanging around together, was RockaBilly, the rough, Blues-influenced Rock'n'Roll developed by former and future Country music yodellers and taken to it's zenith by Elvis. Little did I realize that day in

1959, goofing in the small pavilion at Mountain Park across Concession Street from Walt's, that our priorities were about to change for a lifetime.

Richard strode up. He'd just got back from a shopping trip to Buffalo with his parents. And he had a gift for me. That day in Mountain Park, Richard gave me my first Little Walter record. My first Chicago Blues recording: "Break It Up" backed with "Me & Piney Brown," Checker 938, 45 rpm, straight from Ross' Rhythm Land on William Street in Buffalo. Otis Spann on piano. Luther Tucker on guitar. Those jumpin' grooves, both sides a musical mind-fuck for a young teen back then. Both tunes still stand out today. I've loved the Blues ever since. Goodbye to the Rock'n'Roll of the Vincents and the Jerry Lees and Little Richard and Chuck. Hello Chicago, electric heartland of the Blues, home to Chess and Vee Jay and Parrot and States Records. Much later in the '80s during an interview with legendary Canadian Blues deejay Daddy Cool, Richard said that hearing Little Walter's first Checker Records' hit "Juke," #758 and recorded way back in 1952, is what inspired him to play harmonica.

Another little fact we didn't know at the time, "Juke" was such a massive R&B and Blues hit in black America (*Blues With A Feeling: The Little Walter Story, Routledge*) that Little Walter was already a legend and had starred at the Apollo Theatre in Harlem, New York City in 1953 and '54.

Our minds were opened by that one recording. We soon discovered that every major and some not so major American cities with indigenous black populations had artists making records for the local Rhythm'n'Blues market using local studios and record labels. The demand for recordings was driven by musicians playing local gigs and if people got into some of the artist's original tunes it was, can we please have a record of it to take home? Rural artists with followings at crossroads juke joints went on to hit nearby cities, doing the same thing: make records for the juke boxes down at the local corner joint so their audience could hear their favourite tunes while the musicians were away playing some other town. Guys like singer/guitarist Frankie Lee Sims would go to Ace Records out of Jackson, Mississippi and of course Sam Phillips at Sun Records in Nashville was recording tons of people and making records for this market too but there wasn't a white, mass market for this music until Elvis and Johnny Cash and Jerry Lee and the rest of the RockaBilly dudes came along. Up in Hamilton we dug the RockaBilly. Richard and I were both still hooked on Rhythm'n'Blues, the black Rock'n'Roll. Hell, I am to this day, but after hearing Little Walter we craved that Blues sound. With that first Chicago Blues recording everything else became secondary.

Blues now ruled
Chess & Vee Jay out of Chicago
Duke out of Houston &
Excello Records out of Nashville

were the main Blues labels we began collecting on future trips to Ross' Rhythm Land Record Store in Buffalo. Ronnie Copple (already playing steel-guitar like Santo & Johnny's "Sleepwalk") Richard and I all became avid collectors. Back when disc jockeys made the hits we listened with reverence to John R. "Down in Dixie" Richbourg and Bill "The Hossman" Allen and Gene Nobles out of WLAC-AM Nashville and George "Hound Dog" Lorenze on WINE-AM and other Buffalo and area AM radio stations. A bonus with WLAC was that the shows we loved on their 50,000 watt signal skipped into Southern Ontario at night, were sponsored by mail order record stores in Tennessee. We could write for catalogues of what they stocked and shipped. One I remember in particular was Randy's Record Shop. Soon we were ordering whatever we wanted and could afford. Original Blues and recent R&B hits. I stuck to Muddy Waters' and Little Walter singles when I had the cash. But we might have to pay extra to get them out of Canadian Customs—*what is this you are importing?*

In the early '50s, Ernie Young, a Nashville businessman, had a chain of jukeboxes and a record store. Discs could be copped by walkin' in or mail orderin' from commercials on Ernie's Record Parade over WLAC, whose mighty wattage could be picked up from Canada to Jamaica, "1510 on EVERYONE'S dial!" Producers would bring in acetates for airplay to check listener response before pressing the records. That's how Chuck Berry's "Maybelline" became a smash. In between pitches for bibles, baby chickens and Royal Crown Hairdressing (so your process wouldn't take a recess), John R. "Way Down in Dixie" Richbourg spun these wanna-be R&B hits. Competition came from Randy's Record Shop in nearby Gallatin, a similar operation founded by Randy Wood, who owned Dot Records.

Their spokesman, Bill "Hoss" Allen, was WLAC's other major deejay that we listened to and idolized.

At home in The Hammer we were ecstatic to find long playing records in Eaton's Department Store. Some of these new-fangled LPs were re-packaged old recordings by
    Elmore James &
    John Lee Hooker &
    more
recorded and released in the early 50's by the pioneering Blues Bihari Brothers out of Culver City, California on the Crown label and these re-releases were very cheap for the time, less than half the price of major label disks.

Our favourite earliest LPs were "The Best of Little Walter" and "The Best of Muddy Waters," two of Chess Records first long playing albums for the rapidly developing 33 1/3 rpm market. The Little Walter album became our bible of what to play, what to sound like as a band and as individuals. When we came to put Son Richard and The Chessmen together the first priority music-wise was to learn all cuts from that album, which we did. The recording still amazes when I throw it on the system today with its sophisticated, awesome grooves.

Junior Teen Town

The Hardtimes dance was chaperoned by Mr. and Mrs. Carter, Mr. Les Patterson, Mr. Lloyd Nancekivel, Mrs. Jane Blandin, Mrs. Cornell and Mrs. Aikens.
This was a special night as there was a band on hand to provide the music. The band was Justice Russ and the Majestics.
Mr. and Mrs. Carter are the parents of one of the band members. Prizes for the night were won by Ray Coulson, Katy Aikens, Carol Grant, Carol Ferguson, John Donnelly and Jane Revill. There was a big turnout of young people. Mr. Millard called time at 10 p.m. as usual but allowed them to dance a bit more.

The late '50s produced Rock'n'Roll tunes that still hit my turntable today. They were debated, danced to, compared and tested over and over again by kids like me and Richard, Ronnie Copple and our peers with similar musical tastes all over North America and declared instant classics. We were hungry to evaluate the music in the Rock'n'Roll and Blues genres, to deem what was worthy to collect and treasure, and eventually, even more importantly still, to select what we'd play in the band!

Check this best-of list of some of the best of the charted records from 1959:

Stagger Lee—Lloyd Price *
Lonely Teardrops—Jackie Wilson
Poison Ivy—The Coasters *
Hey Little Girl—Dee Clark
So Fine—The Fiestas
What A Difference A Day Makes—Dinah Washington
There Goes My Baby—The Drifters
Sea of Love—Phil Phillips *
Try Me—James Brown *
You Got What It Takes—Marv Johnson
Smoke Gets In Your Eyes—The Platters
The Twist—Hank Ballard & the Midnighters *
That's Why—Jackie Wilson
Charlie Brown—The Coasters
You're So Fine—The Falcons *
It's Just A Matter Of Time—Brook Benton
I Cried A Tear—LaVern Baker
Kansas City—Wilburt Harrison *
Pretty Girls Everywhere—Eugene Church
I Only Have Eyes For You—The Flamingos
I Wanna' Walk You Home—Fats Domino

and that's only the tip of the iceberg. There was Elvis and Chuck and a ton of Blues that never got near the pop charts and then out of all that came a song that changed musical styles and started Rock'n'Roll down a long evolving path away from the Rock'n'Roll shuffle to Rock&Soul and Punk and Funk and on and on and on and on—

The tune: Ray Charles' "What'd I Say" *
Brother Ray.

What did you say
yes indeed.

* indicates a song done live by Son Richard & The Chessmen at some time

Goin Down To William Street

1959, yeah, 16 years old, just read Kerouac's *On The Road*, got my thumbs out and I'm headin' for the Red-White-and-Blue. America. Specifically, Buffalo, New York, to check out black culture first hand and bring back home as much black vinyl Blues as I need, or can carry, to keep that soul feeling alive and my happy feet dancin' till the next time I cross border.

    Black Rock'n'Roll was at its peak
    Jackie Wilson—Hank Ballard—Brook Benton—Dinah Washington—Marv Johnson
    Little Jr. Parker—Little Willie John ... *the list goes on & on*
    In what was the climax of a great musical year

The international Peace Bridge between Fort Erie, Ontario and Buffalo, New York

COOL FOOL

Ray Charles released "What'd I Say? Parts 1 & 2," the groove changing tune that broke from the 2/4 shuffle that had dominated R&B and pop since Louis Jordan and the post-WW II swing era. Charles opened the way for James Brown and The Famous Flames *Live At the Apollo*, 1963 and by '65 James had arrived on the pop charts all over the planet with the mega-hit "Papa's Got a Bran' New Bag." The new generation up and comers wanted to play the new Soul music and "blue-eyed Soul" became a staple of the Toronto and local music scene in a way that still hasn't changed. Not entirely. But that was later. Yeah, later.

Back then:
> *See the girl with the red dress on*
Every band I knew had to try it out.
> *She can shake that thing all night long*
ALL NIGHT LONG! A challenge! A dare!
> *Wha'd I say?*
A dare sent out to every red-blooded adolescent male in North America.
> *Tell me wha'd I say?*
Even in Canada we got it. We knew what he'd said.
> *Uunnnnngh...Ohhhhh...*
> *Unnngh...Ohh...Ungh-Oh...Ungh-Oh...Ungh-Oh WOW!!!*
> *Tell me wha'd I say?*
He said if you wanted success…
> *See the girl with the diamond ring*
then you better get out there and shake your thing. ALL NIGHT LONG.

For us that meant heading to Buffalo, the biggest centre of culture around Lake Ontario. Back then Buffalo was still a thriving, inventive, manufacturing centre with a booming economy that supported universities, music halls, professional theatre, art galleries, architectural wonders and most of all, professional musicians. When midnight blue laws turned Hamilton bars into hollow pumpkins, jive-foxes and howlin' wolves moved down the Quick and Easy Way, across the Peace Bridge and into The Queen City where the night and the life lasted well into the wee small hours.

In the '50s and early '60s Toronto was still emerging from its history as a colonial backwater in the British Empire, loyal to the Crown and proud of its place in the Commonwealth, the place had been dominated by dour Scots since long before Confederation. Until the 1960s the most culturally significant event in Toronto had been when loyalist louts dumped upstart publisher and rebel Billy McKenzie's type-cases into the city's harbour. That had been in 1826.

Sure, there was change, starting with the opening of The O'Keefe Centre, owned and operated by its namesake brewery but it was still another decade before Ontario's beer halls combined their sparsely decorated "Men" and "Ladies and Escorts" rooms, making room for bandstands. Prior to 1970, decent Ontario women who wanted a drink in their own company had to quench their thirst at home.

Henry Moore's "The Archer" would not land in Nathan Phillips Square until 1966 after first being rejected by city fathers, and the "earth-to-city-council" space station, new City Hall itself, had opened only a year earlier. Mies van der Rohe's slabs would not grace a downtown banker's block until 1967. Seiji Ozawa would not take up the baton of the Toronto Symphony Orchestra until 1965. And the monthly urban-culture magazine Toronto Life did not publish until 1966. Before then the magazine's titular words had widely been considered antonyms.

But Arkansas RockaBilly entertainer Rompin' Ronnie Hawkins had already plowed his first furrow through Ontario, combining white Country with black Blues, starting in Hamilton's Golden Rail. The year was 1958 and Hawkins whetted the appetite of every city kid sporting a pack of Export A's rolled in the sleeve of his white T-shirt. Where to get more? Where to get the original Blues?

Sure, as part of the Folk Music movement Toronto helped to revive the careers of many Blues players including '50s electric Blues cats Jimmy Reed, Muddy Waters, John Lee Hooker and whoever they could find still playing from the pre World War II era, preferably while being accompanied by acoustic guitar. But almost as close and in the opposite direction, Buffalo had the real thing on a regular basis, plus

American beer
Thunderbird wine
Toasted tobacco cigarettes
  Rich loved his 'Kents' with the charcoal filter
  I preferred king-sized, plain-ended Pall Malls
& beer with less alcohol than Canadian brews
so we could drink more
a lot more &
legal drinking age was only 18 &
liquor was available all over the place
from corner stores to super markets &
it was so much cheaper
everybody went to the wild & woolly Niagara Frontier to party & drink

And everything else seemed so much cheaper too, especially cool-looking shoes and boots in hip styles unknown in Hamilton. We'd slide into the downtown Thom McAnns for a pair of what we called Spanish Boots back then, nose-pickers with pointy toes, vamps up over the ankles and 1 ½" heels. In the mid '60s they came back into style and were known as Beatle Boots (Wonder why?) and available all over but when we wanted them you could only find 'em States' side. Most entertainment and fashion was slow getting to Canada back then, so:

we bought their records
we listened to their radio stations
we watched their TV channels
we partied in their clubs
oh & don't forget the slick shirts

Okay, okay. Toronto *did* have its black music subculture in those days plus now and again acts brought in from the States would turn up in some rockin' Rhythm'n'Blues dance hall in a low-rent neighbourhood. Acts like Bobby Blue Bland, pre-Soul James Brown (he was a mighty rocker before all that soul stuff). But the occurrence of shows was unreliable and the atmosphere often precious and self-aware when it wasn't out and out rough and nasty.

Dig: *Jimmy Reed playin' at one of these TO dancehalls*
        we all wanted to go
        we all had to go
        we knew all his tunes
        we'd collected all his records
        we took the bus down & followed the crowd
        to a dance hall somewhere around Sunnyside

After a warm-up act (and I can't even remember who that was except they were white and had a three piece horn line) Jimmy was brought out on stage.
        they lowered his microphone
        they sat him in a chair
        they handed him his guitar
        he opened his mouth to sing
        he was pissed out of his mind
Jimmy Reed, *you name 'em I'll play 'em*, but his wife Mary came out and sat beside him and started whispering in his ear, sometimes singing aloud giving Jimmy the lyrics. Somehow they made something of Jimmy's hit tunes. What the hell, that was the real Jimmy Reed. At least we can say we saw him live.

But Buffalo was still a party goin' on, man, low-down and dirteeeeeeeeeeeeeeeeee. Even the cops wore uniforms splotched with coffee and gravy and who knew what else. Buffalo was blue-collar, a steel city like Hamilton, the inner city filled with examples of extraordinary architecture from earlier, wealthier times but already starting to fray at the edges. Downtown was grimy as all get out:
        litter
        industrial waste
        phone booths reeking of piss
        people sleeping on the sidewalks
        cigarette butts everywhere.

Hamilton wouldn't hit those lows for another twenty years or more. Welcome boy to this-ain'-Canada. Buffalo had peaked and although we didn't know it back then, was already on its way out.

Canada was still so tight and nice and polite. Even the cops were polite back then. People still lined up for everything—
> *Excuse me…&*
> *I'm sorry, did I take your place?*
They got dressed up to go shopping downtown.
> *Thank you…&*
> *You're welcome*
It was an act of defiance to spit on the street or throw an apple core out a car window.

The Cool Fool circa 1960

Buffalo was the dirtiest city I'd ever seen and seemed all the more big-city sophisticated for it. The dirt in Buffalo worked its way into border customs, dick-heads in charge of keeping bad-actor kids from their "pristine" shores—
> *filthy brown uniforms*
> *shitty brown attitude*
> *big-ass pistols slung under protruding bellies*
> *ready to put the fear of America into our young Canadian bones*
In those pre-computer days they'd get up in your face and accuse you of all kinds of shit, vagrancy, car theft, street pissing, pud pulling.
> *That stuff ain't allowed here, you know it?*
Accuse you of having the same name as one of their most-wanted, master criminals.
> *You sure that ain't you, boy? You sure look like him.*
Or they'd keep you waiting around while they pretended to call your home-town cops and check for your criminal record.

Later, after having travelled through several European countries during the '60s I still thought the guards at the Peace Bridge to Buffalo and at Windsor/Detroit too, were the nastiest bunch of border bullies you'd ever want to mess with. But it was worth it to get to William Street.

There were seven or eight of us who hung out together because of our love of RockaBilly and R&B. That was our gang. In 1959 we began hitch-hiking to Buffalo regularly, weather permitting, for cheap smokes, the occasional bottle of Thunderbird Wine and most important, those recordings impossible to get anywhere in Canada. But we'd heard them on the radio on WINE-AM 1080 Buffalo (a station so small that it ran down at sundown) and we'd bin' told by the radio man that we could get

> *the same tunes you're hearin' right here at*
> *Ross The Square Toss Boss' Rythmn Land*
> *down on William Street or*
> *at Audrie's over on Jefferson Avenue…*

both stores located at that time in the heart of Buffalo's black neighbourhood.

Bad lookin' dudes hanging out in the doorways of bars and garages and barber shops, eyeballin' our scared, skinny, white asses all the way from Downtown to Ross'. Signs in every available window proclaiming:

> *Coming To Town:*
> *JAMES BROWN!*
> *HANK BALLARD!*
> *BOBBY BLAND!*
> *JIMMY SMITH!*
> THE FIVE BLIND BOYS
> *COME! SEE! HEAR!*

Flippin' out, seein' these cats in the doorways, jukebox jivin' with long-neck bottles held loose in their hands, Chuck Berry wailin' "Someday your name'll be in lights, sayin' Johnny B. Goode tonight!" from the interior of dark bars.

And that was in the morning, unheard of in puritan Ontario.

Making it to Ross' at last. What a chill, looking at those hand-lettered and often misspelled "new-release" signs hangin' from strings in the front window.
> *Hey!*
> *Dig it!*
> *Buy It!*
> *Hot From The Factory*
> *Fresh On The Charts*
> *Elmore James: "The Sky Is Crying"*
> *Inside Right Now!*

And inside: racks and racks of dusty records. Boxes of records. Unknown records. Rockin' records. Want em' records. Gotta have 'em records. And racks of records Ross wouldn't even let us look through, as much as we would beg, they looked so fine.
> *Hey Ross, can I use the toilet? Long walk uptown, you know?*
> *Yeah, sure. Okay*

Toilet in this warehouse-like room behind the storefront and it was FILLED with racks and racks of old Zoot Suits from the '40s. Old cameras and gear and all sorts of outdated merchandise. Plus a ton of old 78s, stacks of wax that we wanted to buy but wouldn't for fear of breaking them on the highway back home.

Home: Two hours later, headin' back uptown loaded with three-for-a-dollar jukebox records, used and washed and sometimes worn and warped but still, always great—and those same cats still out there, hangin' from cracked door frames, drinkin', jivin' and livin' the Blues.

Home: Most times having spent our return fare and the last bus gone anyway, walking across the Peace Bridge to hitch from Fort Erie, Canada Customs almost waving us on through:
> *Get these kids back across the border quick*

Home: about 85 miles away.

Hitchhiking by the side of the highway, the sun setting after a fine March day but the temperature dropping and now it looks like fog coming in off Lake Erie, creepin' down the Niagara River, rolling up and across the QEW, a chill setting in the bones and my last dime gone on Texas Red Hots, Pall Malls and well-grooved vinyl. Not a car in sight.

Borders are a fact of life, sources of opportunity and regret for those who live near them. People from the Golden Horseshoe, wrapped around the west-end of Lake Ontario, still go to Buffalo and Western New York to hunt up name-brand goods at cheap prices, inexpensive meals and other American bargains from the Land of Cotton. But the steel plants have moved away, manufacturing shifting south, then further south again, then chasing cheap wages so far west they've reached the Far East. There's still great architecture all over the old city of Buffalo, including examples of Frank Lloyd Wright and great modern art at the Albright-Knox Art Gallery, but a lot of buildings are empty, people, those who could afford it, having moved to white-bread suburbs.

Still there is 11 hours of Blues every weekend from the University of Buffalo radio station, WBFO-FM 88.7 and these days you can find Blues Saturday nights on two stations out of Toronto. Couple of times a year a major act will show up in The Queen City and places like the Lafayette Tap Room blow Blue all the time but there's action every bit as lively now in TO. You can still find way more Blues releases old and new and books on the Blues too in Buffalo but they're now found at chain-owned book/music stores in strip-malls out on perimeter roads. The only things still the same are those border bullies guarding American shops from Canucks with bucks. Buffalo is nostalgia now. Old times.

Ross' Rhythm Land record shop on William Street, Buffalo, New York.

Best Damn Blues Band In The World!

Richard Newell didn't go to Hill Park Secondary School on the Mountain with the rest of us. He was very talented at painting and drawing and qualified for Central High School's visual arts program. The school was mid-block on Wentworth St. N. between Cannon and Barton and man the location was bad territory back then! Richard had to dodge the local street gang, a group of thugs that called themselves the Wentworth Street Flyers. No pistols like today, just baseball bats and chains and knuckle-dusters and sometimes zip guns but that seemed serious enough at the time. Also at Central High were other early Hamilton rockers such as Rick Golka (local king of the Fender Telecaster, pre- Robbie Robertson) and Nelson Flowers (drummer and later vocalist for the then trend setting Bishops).

Meanwhile, back on the Mountain, I was learning some basic guitar technique from two brothers who had moved into newly built apartments on Concession Street over by Mountain Park. When I say "basic" I mean, real basic: E, A & G. These guys were from England, their father having been transferred by his employer to a branch in The Hammer. We'd see each other around the park, going and coming from school and eventually we chatted. It turned out the older one, Pat, was a big fan of something called "Skiffle" in England, especially Lonnie Donegan who'd recently had hits with a great acoustic up-tempo version of "Rock Island Line" and the novelty tune "Does Your Chewing Gum Lose It's Flavour (On The Bed Post Overnight?)" Younger brother Micky was into Buddy Holly and The Everly Brothers which I knew all about! Soon I was learning to pick tunes like "Tom Dooley" by the Kingston Trio. There was some pressure for me to sing as well, as the brothers desperately wanted to do three-part harmony. So I got some guitar lessons and eventually an acoustic guitar to fool around on. After a couple of years the brothers' father got transferred again and I've never seen or heard from them since. But the die was cast.

According to old album cover notes written by Dave Booth, Richard started playing the harmonica in the early '60s. There were no other local harp players around at the time, someone to go and watch and learn from. The only "how to play" harmonica instruction books he could find in area music stores were not about playing the Blues. So Rich just kept listening to his records and taught himself by trying to play along. This led to a couple of early missteps. The first arose when Richard saw a picture of Little Walter (Jacobs) posing with a chromatic harmonica on the cover of his first Chess album. Richard thought that the Chicago Blues singer played that type of instrument on all his recordings. Later Richard discovered that Walter used the cheaper, non-chromatic Marine Band harp on most of his records, so Richard went out and purchased one.

But you know how you sometimes see Blues harp players with belts of Marine Bands hanging from their torsos or with their harps carefully arranged on a stool nearby? It's because Marine Band harps play in fixed keys. This led to Richard's second misstep. The only Marine Band harp Richard was able to obtain locally was in the key of C. I remember being in Ann Foster Music downtown on King East with Rich ogling the few harmonicas inside a glass display case. The upshot was Rich had to learn to play the Blues "cross harp" style, meaning whatever key the song was in, for example C, the harmonica to be used would be in the fifth, G.

A lot of Little Walter stuff was in the Keys of A, D and E but Richard had the opposite, a harp in the key of C meaning that he could only play along with records in the key of G. "Going to New Orleans" by Jesse and Buzzy on the Savoy label was the only record he owned that fit the bill and that's where he started. Richard has said that it took him two years of practicing the harmonica before he considered himself a good player.

38

In the very early sixties Hamilton had a small number of Rock'n'Roll bands. One, The Barons, was a Mountain group, playing only instrumentals. Ronnie Copple, Andy Torkelson, Steve Caskenette on guitar, Richie Hodgson on drums. They practiced at Brucedale Fish & Chips, a shop owned by Copple's parents on the north side

Basement Blues: Babe Myles, Ron Copple, Steve Caskenette (in front) Richard Newell, Doug Carter (in back)

of Brucedale Avenue between East 13th and 14th. Two doors west on the corner of East 13th was our neighbourhood soda bar with jukebox hangout, The Rocket. The band took over the chippie Fridays after the fryers were turned off, usually about 7:00 p.m. Weekends in a working town often began with take-away, grocery shopping and then go out and so-cial-ize, maybe skip the groceries till Saturday ayem. Anyway, going to different schools, even Richard's best friends hadn't known that he'd been studying the harp until he up and announced that he had joined The Barons as lead vocalist and harmonica player. Were we amazed? You bet your duck-ass hair do! Even more astounding was the news he would be playing with the band downtown at the Jet Restaurant the upcoming Friday night. On the west side of James Street just north of King, The Jet was one of the few places downtown that would let teens hang around drinking cokes and playing the jukebox all night so it seemed natural they would try a band in there. Of course the whole gang showed up and damn if it wasn't pretty good. And very cool!

It turned out the band had ambitions and was looking to add a bass player for a fuller, more "Official" sound. Five guys playing music wasn't a proper band until they had a bass and The Barons' rhythm guitar player wasn't willing to make the switch. It just wasn't cool back to then to play bass when you might be a hot shot guitar player some day—or already were in your mind. Richard suggested this friend of his who dug the music and who'd been messing with an acoustic guitar and trying to sing third in three part harmony; a guy by the name of Doug Carter. I was invited to the "chip store" the next Friday. Steve Caskenette had me fool around on his guitar and saw I could pick out some basic bass lines. He showed up at my place a few days later with a sales pitch. I should buy an electric bass and an amplifier and join the band.

Oh boy, this meant a lot of begging and crying around the Carter household. The Hammer was a blue-collar town, its Mountain surveys populated by hard-working families squeezing pennies out of weekly pay cheques to raise their kids away from the lower city. My parents didn't have much money but they did have three more kids. Maybe this is where I really learned to cry the Blues. Eventually my grandfather came through.

Thanks, Grandad.

Downtown to Pilgrim's Music Store, where hip musicians from all over Ontario shopped when they were playing in The Hammer. Located on the east side of Catherine Street between King and King William, Pilgrim's salesman in charge of electric stuff was Bobby Pedlar, father of current #1 and

The Rocket Soda Bar and Brucedale Fish and Chips buildings as they are today.

future Hamilton Hall of Musical Fame drummer, song writer, humourist, vocalist and local legend Jack Pedlar. Jack came by the life honestly, his old man, Bobby, having played with a number of big name Swing bands in his younger days and was at that time very active on the local music scene and in the then still powerful musicians union local. My grandfather hadn't given me enough money for a Fender Precision or Jazz Bass but Bobby picked me out a very nice semi-acoustic Kay Bass and an early Gibson bass amp with a 12" speaker. I still have and play my Kay today and as a historical note, Bobby Washington, bass player extraordinaire of the Bishops and member of Hamilton's famous musical Washington family, also played a Kay back then.

Rick Golka

Kays are very interesting early electric instruments. Being semi-acoustic as opposed to solid body like the Fender basses, they are very pluckable and slapable in a stand-up bass way. Stand-up acoustic basses were hard to amplify back in the '50s which meant they couldn't match the volume of amplified lead and rhythm electric guitars, drums pounding away behind them. Using a semi-hollow body bass like the Kays let the bass players keep up with the volume needed to be heard and also apply some of that stand-up bass playing technique when covering older R&B, Blues and RockaBilly favourites. But as the electric guitar and amp got bigger and louder the solid body bass took over completely.

With a new front man and a bass-anchored Blues orientation The Barons quickly became The Chessmen featuring Son Richard (Newell), attracting pianist/manager Paul Cronkwright. The new name was taken to honour Chess Records, the Chicago-based company that recorded so many of the musicians who influenced us. Our repertoire in the beginning leaned heavily to

41

COOL FOOL

Jimmy Reed, Elmore James and the Excello Records sound of Lonesome Sundown, Lazy Lester and Slim Harpo, Blues styles that are easiest to play when you're starting out. As the band matured we added the more sophisticated Chicago stylings of Muddy Waters and Little Walter along with some of our favourite Rock'n'Roll numbers and any current hits that sounded even slightly bluesy.

As the band rolled along Richard continued to add more and more harp tunes like those on records by Jr. Wells, Sonny Boy Williamson II and Little Jr. Parker to his repertoire.

After months of rehearsals, several nights a week, The Chessmen started playing "out" in early 1962 at dances in school gyms, community centres and parties. Audiences were small but enthusiastic. Our first big step was to play the hottest dance on the Mountain and one of the best in the city. This was the Mountain YM-YWCA on Upper Wellington, right in our backyard, but they booked mostly out-of-town acts, especially from Toronto. We knew the guys running the weekly Saturday night gig from around the neighbourhood. Still, it took a lot of effort to get the booking.

The date came, we showed and set up, the kids packed in, we started the first set and the gig is goin' good, real good, everyone dancin' and jivin' to our tunes and already it's break time. The band is in a dressing room provided but, like,
>*where's Richard?*
>*Nowhere to be seen*

It's getting past time to play again when the Y staff advisor, the head guy, shows up with Richard in tow. Son is accused of
>*...drinking.*
>*God forbid!*
>*Beer in the Young Men's CHRISTIAN Association.*
>*Uh oh!*

They let us finish the night under a close eye and then delivered a second lecture with our pay at the end of it. We were kids. If any of us drank it was an isolated lark so far as we knew, but looking back, that Y gig was the first inkling that Richard needed a beer or two to get up on stage and "do it," perform in public. Of course that was the last time we ever played the Y.

BANNED FOR LIFE

Band for life banned for life, The original Chessmen:
Steve Caskenette, Richie Hodgson, Richard Newell, Doug Carter, Ron Copple

Yeah so, lots more gigs out there
Dances everywhere

Shortly thereafter Steve Caskenette left The Chessmen to go out on the club circuit as local singer Frank Rondell's lead guitar. Rick Golka was brought in to replace him. Rick had played with Frank earlier in his career and had cut a couple of sides with Frank. The one tune "Someone Like You" backed with Carl Perkins' "Your True Love" got some minor airplay in the area. Ronnie Hawkins later did a quite successful version of "Someone Like You."

Fall of 1963 we got an even bigger break. The Sportsmen's Lanes and Lounge was our biggest gig to date. It was a huge bowling alley financed by players from the local Tiger Cats football club. Perched on the side of the escarpment, top of Wentworth Street, you could look down on the city lights from the parking lot at a time when King and James was the centre of our universe. Summers, bowling leagues over, lanes on one side were covered with boards and a big stage raised at back where the pins normally set up. Best of all it had an acoustic piano that was reasonably in tune. Bonus! Paul Cronkwright could join us on keyboards. Sunday nights the floor was packed with kids ready to shake their things. They came from all over the city to be seen and to boogie to their favourite bands, the biggest names around town and bands from as far away as Toronto and there we were,
> *Son Richard & The Chessmen*
> *First timers from the Mountain*
> *Were we gonna' cut it with the kids?*
> *Can we make these people dance?*
> *Everybody starin' at us waiting to see what we're gonna do.*
> > *Don't worry about it guys, everything is gonna' be alright*
> *& we went into our signature lead-off song,*
> *Howlin' Wolf's "House Rockin' Boogie"*
> > *Good evenin' everybody—Son Richard is in your town!*

Like other local vocalists, Rich sang and played through a guitar amp back then. It would be years yet before Toronto's Pete Traynor came up with a reasonably priced portable

PA system designed for vocals (an amplifier with several inputs for microphones and 2 independent speaker units that stood 4 to 6 feet tall at each side of the stage.) When we first played The Sportsmen's we made do with whatever we could afford and could get our hands on. It was about the commitment, not the equipment, confirmed for us in '64 seeing Muddy Waters' band's beat-out amps, some with makeshift clothesline-wire handles, and his band's battered guitars that had been manhandled in and out of countless pawnshops. So we weren't ashamed to improvise. Cronkwright liberated some microphones out of payphone handsets, strung them together and taped them across the soundboard, hooking it all up to an amp. I played my Kay through the Gibson, Rick Golka had a Telecaster and a Fender amp of some sort and I think Russell Carter,

who had joined us for the gig that night, played a Goya at that time, a wicked looking gold-spangled axe but I don't remember his amplifier. And The Sportsmen's rocked. Well if you can't dance to the Blues then you can't dance. Yeah, they rocked all night, and we were asked back!

But it was still hard to convince the people that booked bands in the city that local talent was as good as anything from away. Still, in the winter of '64-65 The Chessmen managed to play at five different area high schools which was considered quite a coup for a Hamilton band back then. We were also regulars at Huntington Park Community Centre, Onteora Public School on the Mountain, the Normanhurst Community Centre on Barton

Normanhurst Community Centre as it is today.

Street in the east end and the Glanbrook Community Centre in Mt. Hope. Around this time The Chessmen's lineup changed again. Right after Steve Caskenette was replaced by Rick Golka from Central High, Richie Hodgson also left to get married and settle down with John "Babe" Myles coming in on drums. In early 1965 Ron Copple left his steel guitar behind and took over the lead guitar role.

To all of us in the band, The Bishops played the best music in town. The group consisted of Russell Carter, guitar, Bobby Washington, bass, Nelson Flowers, drums and Harrison Kennedy, vocals. Then one day it was Russ and Bobby with Ron Knappet on drums and Nelson was fronting the group. A story went around that Harrison and Nelson had been in a bitter physical struggle to determine who would front the Bishops. I never did find out if that

The Bishops at the Downstairs: Bobby Washington, Ron Knappett, Nelson Flowers, Russell Carter

was true, but it's a great story. Eventually Harrison went on to a very successful recording career with The Chairmen of the Board on Invictus Records out of Detroit. But that was later. One of the Bishops first regular gigs had been the Teen Town Dance upstairs at the old Dundas Town Hall. They walked to their first date there, carrying their equipment from the north end of Hamilton out King Street West all the way to downtown Dundas. Must have been ten miles. That's dedication. It wasn't long before those cats were hot on the jumpin' and jivin' Hamilton scene They were a staple at The Downstairs on McNab Street. Opening for the "name" band at the Saturday night gigs playing until the bars closed at midnight and the band chosen to play the club that night showed up.

The Bishops became our mentors. They'd already been around a few years playing a mix of Blues ala Jimmy Reed, James Brown, Bobby Blue Bland, Bo Diddley etc. and they kept adding the latest Rhythm'n'Blues hits as they came out. Sometimes there was a little Jazz thrown in. I loved it when Reggie Washington was available for keyboards and he played "Blues In The Closet." I don't know where they picked up their version but I've since found a great rendition by Thelonious Monk to remember it by. Eventually I had the privilege, several times, to fill in for Bobby Washington on an early set at The Downstairs while The Bishops' bassist finished working the 3 to 11 shift at Stelco. Sometimes, if The Bishops had another gig, The Chessmen got the call to do the opening gig at the Downstairs. When we needed a fill in lead player we'd call on Russell Carter. We all became good friends. It was members of both bands hopped the bus to Toronto, going to see Jimmy Reed that time I already mentioned. Hell, both bands had many of Jimmy's tunes in their repertoires.

> *Jimmy Reed:*
> *18 records on the Billboard/Cashbox R&B charts, '58 through '63*
> *"Bright Lights Big City" one of three in '61 to break into the pop charts*
> *Formative years for me,*
> > *for Richard,*
> > *for Ron Copple*
> *For the musical direction of The Chessmen.*

The Bishops greatest gig, at least in terms of publicity, was a marathon at Lakeland Pool in July 1964. Lakeland was a large pool and hall by Hamilton's Beach Strip on the shores of Lake Ontari-ari-ario. The gig was a pre-Guinness Book of Records type of endurance contest to break the 80-hour continuous playing record of the time and damn if the Bishops didn't do it and set a new record. The whole scheme was set up and promoted by the hottest disc jockey in The Hammer, wild and crazy Dave Mickie, during his brief run at radio station CHIQ. In the age of motor-mouthed radio DJs Mickie's engine ran on pure nitro. In the '50s he fronted The Revols, a band that featured Richard Manuel, later with The Band. Rock'n'Roll chaos personified, on air and at public appearances, Mickie mangled un-recorded sponsor commercials until clients cried and Mickie got fired. But screwing with all that carefully-worded, manipulative bumpf made him a hero to local teens, the intended targets of those would-be-slick commercials and Mickie would quickly re-appear at another radio station, probably at higher pay and bringing a bigger audience in his wake each time. One of his more infamous and outrageous stunts was landing a helicopter in the playing field behind my old high school, Hill Park, just as students headed home for the day.

> *Dave Mickie's here*

Left: Bobby Washington, Nelson Flowers, Russell Carter at CHIQ's Lakeland Pool Marathon Challenge of the Year, July 1964

What?
Dave Mickie's here
Where?
He just landed in a helicopter
No shit! Lemme at him!

Whichever way was home, kids changed direction and raced to embrace the radio jock. And it was great, Mickie mobbed by 1,000 or more, signing autographs, shaking hands, high fiving, the perfect photo-op until a slightly off-kilter non-student weilding a bicycle chain had to be warned to "keep away" by a phalanx of the school's football team acting as bodyguards to the diminutive DJ. The attacker skirmished with police and was arrested. Two radio-station secretaries were injured in the crush to connect with Mickie and a death threat was phoned into the station next day. "When I get to these things," Mickie later told The Spec, "all I see is a sea of faces, hollering and shouting and people trying to reach my clothes."

Mickie left CHIQ in September, but he hosted Hamilton television's *Club 11 Dance Party* for the following season and *Music Hop* for CBC after that, before again revolutionizing FM rock radio in the '80s as programming director at CFNY in Brampton. Little was heard of the attacker again except that much later I was told he had briefly been a children's counsellor at the aforementioned YM-YWCA, the one where Richard had been chastised for drinking. Man.

That was Rock'n'Roll
That was Dave Mickie
That was the influence of Top 40 Radio

Things were definitely changing in Ontario. In 1962 Sam the Record Man opened in Toronto and a good variety of Blues, Jazz and Rock records started to become available in Canada at last! In '63 Toronto's Ritchie Knight and The Midnights recorded "Charlena." It reached number one on Toronto's highly influential CHUM-AM 1050 play-list. Ritchie and the band became very popular, playing Hamilton often. This was even before Canadian content rules boosted play by Canuck musicians on Canuck radio stations. Ironically, those rules could have meant less play time for the US Blues recordings we all loved. Thanks to Nevin Grant over at Hamilton's CKOC who kept slippin' some black hits from the States in with the regular, watered down "Bobby Who" music that otherwise got charted and played over and over and over again. And in 1964 The Hawks left Ronnie Hawkins and set out on their own as Levon Helm and The Hawks featuring Robbie Robertson. We got to see them in what would have been one of their first gigs when they played The Grange Tavern. Wow what a fresh, new sound!

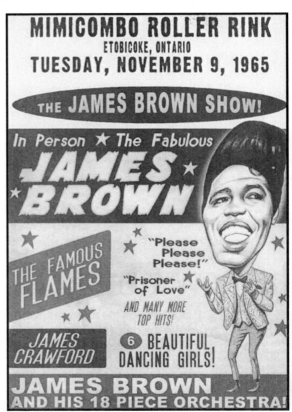

-source unknown

Other big-time acts influential on the Hamilton music scene in the early '60s played at The Silhouette Club, corner of Main Street East and Walnut South. By '64 this included Canadian groups like David Clayton Thomas and The Shays and The Five Rogues later becoming the Mandala featuring Dominic Troianno. Occasionally The Silhouette brought in US acts that were playing Toronto, often from Ronnie Hawkins' Yonge St. Le Coq d'Or Tavern—The Cock Door, get it?—that too were looking for that extra cash from a Sunday night gig. So we got to see

> Bo Diddley &
> The Ike & Tina Turner Revue
> Live!
> Fan-tastic!

We loved Tina from the get-go. Hadn't even seen her famous legs in the flesh, but we'd heard those fabulous pipes on "A Fool In Love" and several other 45s from that period. Ike Turner we knew from his all-instrumental, Crown Records album, especially his guitar overview of the history of the Blues: "All the Blues, All the Time." We'd been huge fans of Bo Diddley from his early Checker Records days, especially the tunes with Little Walter playing harp. "Pretty Thing," "Diddley Daddy," "Who Do You Love" and especially "You Don't Love Me (You Don't Care)" from the album *Go Bo Diddley*.

You just gotta' love Walter's harp as he soars on that one and of course there's Bo's awesome and very obscure single "Cops and Robbers" b/w "Down Home Special." Very inspiring to the young Richard Newell and the rest of our band. There are so many more from Bo's first two albums that still cook today. Yeah I know he started to "pop music" out on a couple of the "Go Bo Diddley" tunes and ever after (Bo Diddley Is A Gunslinger) but you gotta credit him that talkin' Blues to a shave-and-a-haircut-two-bits rhythm. Tell me another story Bo Monster!

Schools, community centres, bowling alleys, roller rinks, town halls, bars and clubs, Hamilton had a monster music scene, so much going on and it all helped us grow musically and stay in touch with the ever-changing business. Why should this be? Why should Hamilton be at the heart of this growing Ontario music business and not Toronto or any of the larger or even similarly sized cities in the province? Maybe Hamilton's rocking music scene had something to do with that proximity to Buffalo and the Blues action there. Maybe it was because Hamilton was blue-collar, industrial, the province's and probably the country's biggest concentration of work-all-day, boogie-all-night labourers and a model for the smaller, hard-working and hard-partying mine and mill towns thrown across the country, their workers drawn from all around the world and finding commonality in any music that makes you want to have another drink and forget your cares.

Or maybe it had something to do with the Shermans, who owned both The Downstairs and Jerry's Man Shop on James St. N. at Cannon. Jerry's would fit you out for the best band uniform, suits and shirts and ties, the hippest suits anywhere in the province and at prices that recognized you were buying bulk for the whole band. Jerry knew from slick. He had the look Ontario bands wanted and what their audiences wanted to see them in.

So you're in town for suits, eh?
You got a band?
Any good?
Hey, why not drop over to the Club
Saturday, after hours,
see who's blowing,
I hear The Hawk's in town
Sonny and Brownie
maybe they'll let you sit in a set

Or maybe the city's pre-eminence in the '50s & '60s had something to do with legendary Hamilton booking agent Harold Kudletts. If you had a band and wanted to go on the road and play Ontario's night clubs, it didn't matter where you were from, you first had to go see Harold in his office on the mezzanine at the Royal Connaught Hotel, John and King Streets. You couldn't get regular gigs and make a living as a full time road musician without him. And even if you were the hottest shit in town, to play the bigger and better clubs you first had to prove to Harold you could please crowds and make money for bar owners up in Kirkland Lake, Cochrane, Rouyn-Noranda or some other nowhere club in Northern Ontario. Pitch and polish your act in the face of the regular Friday-night booze-up, don't drink your paycheque away, finish late Saturday night in Cornwall, pack your gear, drive two-lane winter roads and show up on time Monday evening in Fort William Port Arthur (Thunder Bay) and Harold might give you shot at Windsor or Hamilton or London or Kingston and maybe, one day, if you're really good, Toronto. *Help!*

The Chessmen never became one of Kudlett's bar bands. For starters, despite

The Chessmen's business card.

Rhythm and Blues
THE
CHESSMEN
Featuring
Son Richard
HAMILTON, ONT. 385-9497
BUSINESS MANAGER: DOUG CARTER — PHONE

our success in local halls and schools, Son Richard didn't have no showmanship. Like zip. It drove the rest of us nuts. Everyone expected the singer to stand up to sing but Richard sat on a stool or a chair, whatever was available, with his harmonicas laid out on another chair beside him. To make matters worse he didn't talk to the audience but barely. This went on for years. For him it was always about the music, not the performance. Eventually when we played in Europe in '65 he started standing up on a regular basis but he never, ever became much of an onstage talker.

The following is The Chessmen set list circa 1964:

The Chessmen, 1964, wearing Seersucker Jackets with Black Velvet Half Collars from Jerry's Mans Shop, James Street North at Cannon:. From left: Richard Newell, Doug Carter, Babe Myles and Steve Caskenette

House Rockin' Boogie (Howlin' Wolf)
Sweet Home Chicago (Little Jr. Parker)
Money (Barret Strong)
Dust My Blues (Elmore James)
Dizzy Miss Lizzy (Larry Williams)
I Won't Go On (Muddy Waters)
I Can't Hold Out (Elmore James)
You're So Fine (The Falcons)
Ooh Poo Pah Do (Jesse Hill)
Let's Go, Let's Go, Let's Go (Hank Ballard)
Green Onions (Booker T & the M.G.'s)
Last Night (The Mar-Keys)
My Babe (Little Walter)
Baby What You Want Me To Do (Jimmy Reed)
Aw Baby (Little Walter)
Blues With A Feeling (Little Walter)
Mathilda (Cookie & the Cupcakes)
Key To The Highway (Little Walter)
Goodbye Baby (Elmore James)
Hoochie Cootchie Man (Muddy Waters)
Sea Of Love (Phil Phillips)
Unseeing Eye (Sonny Boy Williamson II)
Messin' With The Kid (Jr. Wells)

Sugar Bee (Cleveland Crochet)
Christina (Brownie McGhee)
Sugar Coated Love (Lazy Lester)
Yonders Wall (Elmore James)
You Know I Love You (Lonesome Sundown)
I'm A King Bee (Slim Harpo)
Late, Late In The Evening (Lazy Lester)
I'm In Love Again (Fats Domino)
San-Ho-Zay (Freddy King)
Hide Away (Freddie King)
Ain't That Lovin' You Baby (Jimmy Reed)
Sun Is Shining (Elmore James)
Don't Go (Lonesome Sundown)
They Call Me Lazy (Lazy Lester)
Gonna' Stick To You Baby (Lonesome Sundown)
Wild Cherry (Leroy Washington)
Got You On My Mind (Cookie & the Cupcakes)
That's Alright (Jimmy Rodgers)
Walkin' By Myself (Jimmy Rodgers)
Sexy Ways (Hank Ballard)
Close Up The Backdoor (Cookie & the Cupcakes)
Ooh-Wee (Muddy Waters)

Not a pop-rock tune amongst them. The Chessmen were not your typical Rock'n'Roll dance band of the day. We played harder and hotter, were way more obscure and proud of it!

England Bound

One month of Grade 13 and I'm outta' there and somehow I landed a job in one of the plant offices at Dofasco. Steve's just finished an abortive tour of the Canadian Navy after a few months. Rich is working the only day job he ever had, at the Canadian Tire on Upper James. Ronnie's going to high school and delivering fish and chips 6 nights a week. Babe wants to play drums, never get a day gig and we all want out so let's get on the Ontario bar circuit and go on the road. It's 1964, we've no kids, mortgages, or responsibilities so it's the right time to quit the job and get down to livin' the music, let's hit the Rock'n'Roll highway. Steve finds us an agent and gets us a gig down around Windsor somewhere. Yeah. OK! Six nights a week, rooms and sounds like OK money so let's go. First problem: how do we get there?

duh!
does anybody own a vehicle?
it was unemployment insurance for me after that fiasco
but The Chessmen rolled on

One night at the Grange Tavern. John Newell, Richard's cousin just in from London. The one in the UK. He's living with Rich's family for a year, and filling our heads with the idea that we'd get more gigs as a Blues band in England than we were getting around The Hammer and Southern Ontario where white Pop or Country ruled.

The Chessmen, winter 1964/65

a commitment was made
we were going to England
we would find a way
a plan of action was conceived
I put it into play

By '64 things were changing big time in the music business. The Beatles were it. Who wanted to hear Slim Harpo, Jimmy Reed, Muddy Waters, Howlin' Wolf, Little Walter or Elmore James anymore, never mind Cookie and The Cupcakes or Lazy Lester? Even we, The Chessmen did Buck Owens and Carl Perkins numbers after Richard met the later-to-be Country singer Dave Waco at Canadian Tire on Upper James, the original one behind where Wendy's is now. Waco was into all the latest Country hits and blasts from the Country past so yeah, we were doin' "Act Naturally" and "Honey Don't" way before Ringo and the boys covered them.

I don't know if that counted, but we had always had a strong RockaBilly, Honky Tonk Country streak on top of the black, especially New Orleans Rock'n'Roll, Mississippi /Chicago Blues appetites and meanwhile gigs for straight-ahead rockin' Blues bands were getting scarce around the area. So when Rich's cousin said he thought The Chessmen would go over big with the kids in England where they loved their Blues but few of the bands that tried could play it really well. Remember, many of the early English Invasion bands started out doing white covers of black R&B hits.

So what the hell, we put together a press kit:
> *band photo*

band resume
tape recording
produced by Bob Moody "The Radio Doctor," who had a radio repair shop on John Street North just down from King and the hippest selection of Jazz and Folk vinyl in the city at that time. There weren't many "recording" studios or even decent reel to reel tape recorders

The Chess-men spring 1965: (back) Richard Newell, Andy Torkelson, Richie Hodgson, (front) Doug Carter, Ron Copple

around The Hammer back then, but Bob had really good portable taping equipment that he would take out to gigs and record bands live, mostly for his own pleasure. We had copies made, then found the addresses of London booking agents in the back of the "New Musical Express," an English rock mag available in downtown Hamilton. Off went 30 press kits.

Then nothing
> followed by nothing
> not a word
> then after a while
> a little more nothing
> followed by more nothing again
> then back came a dozen responses
>> show up and we'll see what we can do
>> making no promises

And that was when we heard from Peter Rood. He was an American music agent based out of Western Germany and he guaranteed us work. So we raised our fare. Quit our jobs if we had them. Took jobs if we didn't. To raise the money I landed a job at S. F. Bowser on Sherman Avenue North below Barton. What a strange gig that was. Their historic product was gas pumps for service stations but the gig I got hired on as 'office staff/gofer' was to make self propelled torpedoes for the American Navy, top secret but I passed the security clearance somehow. Go figure. Still innocent times and anyways, anything to get to Europe and rock. We all one way or another raised the coin and off we went. We booked passage on a boat, to keep our axes handy. It was probably cheaper in 1965 that an aeroplane trip. The train to the Montreal docks left from Hamilton's CNR Station on James Street North, now

Ron Copple, April 1965

the labour union banquet hall. Our families came to see us off. Next stop Liverpool.

It was a six to eight day trip back then depending on weather. Rich and I left earlier than the other guys so we could visit family we both had in England: mine in Blackburn, Lancashire and Sidcup, Kent; Rich's in West Ham, East London. Ron, Andy and Babe left a couple of weeks later. We would all meet up at the docks outside Amsterdam where we imagined Rood would be eagerly waiting. So we took the boat-train to Montreal and then the sights down the St. Lawrence were seen mostly through the window of the bar on an ocean liner, albeit a smallish one.

It was a boatload of seniors heading for a last look at their Scottish homeland. We were 21 year old rockers. Naturally we got the worst table in the dining room between the kitchen and the head. It was our first experience with ship-board protocol where you had to eat during your "shift" or go hungry. After a couple of days of struggling to make the meals on time and then being served dead last, Richard took matters into his own hands. He picked up a bun from a basket in the middle of our table and hurled it across the room landing it in the middle of someone else's table. I didn't know whether to shit or chew niblets. I started laughing instead as Richard continued chucking buns about the room. It's possible I chucked a few myself before the episode was over. Needless to say we were,
BANNED FROM THE DINING ROOM!
Oh well, we'd been banned from better joints than this, Christian associations for young men if you'll recall, so we spent the rest of the voyage dining in the bar. Barley sandwich anyone?

That fuckin' boat vibrated 24-7 all 6 days to Liverpool. Sit at the bar and watch your drink jiggle. Don't look down when your pissing either, that water in the bowl is sloshing back and forth back and forth back and forth—uh oh my tummy! Five days out and Richard wakes me up at dawn to watch the north coast of Ireland slide by. Shady. Misty. Rocky. Seagully. Oh did I mention green? Oh yeah, intensely green. Ireland. Later that day we docked at Greenock in Scotland where much to our derision they piped the departing passengers down the gangplank. And then off to Liverpool but first one more night aboard on a storm tossed, foggy Irish Sea. Very scary. Imagine the headlines:
FUTURE BLUES LEGENDS LOST AT SEA.

COOL FOOL

Doug and Richard England bound:
Shipboard antics (top)
Blowin' the harp to celebrate our arrival (middle)
Have Mersey! We're in Liverpool (right)

And then it was morning. Yes oh yes. Open up your eyes and let the sun shine in! We were sailing up the Mersey. Shoutin' "have mercy Miss Percy." Thirty minutes after leaving the boat we were in some basement store buying records. Great Blues stuff we'd never seen. Knocked out. Then there were the 3 chicks dancing in a listening booth to a Muddy Waters record and then to a Howlin' Wolf. Looked like England was the right place for the Blues for sure.

But first we had a holiday. Rich and I spent a week with my relatives in Blackburn, Lancashire who day tripped us around to all the sights. Blackpool and it's famous tower on the beach and it's boardwalk and dance halls and other assorted tourist traps. The Lake District in Cumberland and the home village and home of some poet, Wordsworth or something. Who knew? Beautiful area. Lancaster Castle. Country manors. Perfectly preserved villages from the 1600s. Lots of English history everywhere. One night Rich and I made it into town to a dance and caught some progressive sounding rock band

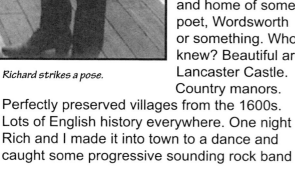

Richard strikes a pose.

Doug on the beach in Blackpool.

This way to London, the original big smoke.

doing a great version of Jimmy Liggins' "Pink Champagne" which turned out to be a clone of Georgie Fame's recently recorded version and more groovy stuff like Mose Allison's "Parchment Farm." Everywhere we looked the kids had long hair down to their shoulders, a style that was just at the beginning of gaining awareness in North America in the summer of 1965.

Next stop Richard's relatives in East London. Canningtown. West Ham. Cockney slang. The same neighbourhood where Richard's parents had run a dancehall before emigrating to Hamilton to open their fish and chippie. Richard's relatives mostly worked in the building trades. Renovation is an ongoing lucrative gig in old European cities with historic architecture of all shapes and sizes and the art of restoration is especially valued. But where I stayed it was just miles and miles of apartment blocks for the poor and the low end working class filling the spaces created by the German bombs of World War 2. These were the kinds of joints they should make the architects live in for a year before they let regular people move in. Then there were the straight out of the sci-fi books giant pod like towers that were scattered about around these apartment complexes. Freaky looking. Apparently some kind of power stations. More like triffids or sumat. Pubs everywhere. People everywhere. More people everywhere. Downtown London and the Soho District were busy all the time but at night when the theatres let out it was sardine city. Spooky for this Hammer boy to be around so many people. Positively claustrophobic.

When we got to England Rich and I learned there was already a "Chessmen" group out of England working Europe. They had a record contract, which meant they were already known, or starting to be. We needed a new name. We worked it out on the bus trip from Blackburn to London. After a bit of head-scratching we were The Good'uns in honour of the Otis Rush Cobra Record tune we so loved, "She's A Good'un."

The summer of '65 and London was a pretty good place to be. Carnaby Street was still hangin' in and the funky Pop-Jazz of Georgie Fame and his Hammond B3 already ruled the underground London dance-club scene and that scene still survives today if you know where to stop, look and listen. On the pop charts The Who's "My Generation" and the "Mod" style were climbing the charts and ready to rule while in the streets, the Elvis-loving "Teds" didn't like it at all. Rumble. Rumble. Rumble. Especially in beach towns.

The music was changing. Again. Already. We got to see lots of good bands, including:
Clapton with John Mayall & The Bluesbreakers
at one of those swing-band type dance halls &
at an outdoor music festival in some big park outside London
it was Long John Baldry's Steam Packet which featured
Rod "The Mod" Stewart on soul vocals &
Reg Dwight (later known as Elton John) on keyboards &
one night we went to see Jimmy James & The Vagabonds
at one of those underground dance clubs
a night of Island Funk & American Soul, horn laden & dark

One day we headed to Bexhill-by-the-Sea where there was a fantastic record shop that from 1958 on had carried all the latest American releases that were unavailable at other record shops in Britain. This was where the early English Blues crowd hung out. They'd train down from London etc., getting hip to the latest grooves, collecting records, exchanging stories, anecdotes and biographical information about the artists they loved to listen to. Out of this had grown a regular publication. "Blues Unlimited" was Mike Leadbitter and John

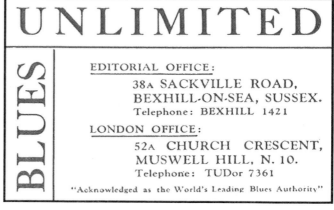

Blues Unlimited business card

Broven who began writing articles in 1963, around the time we somehow found out about it back in The Hammer probably through those same English musical papers we could often get at stands around Gore Park, albeit a week or two late. Knowing about these cats Richard had been exchanging information about the music with Mike Leadbitter since '64 so when Leadbitter and Broven found out we were coming to England, we were invited down to Bexhill-on-the-Sea for the weekend. We had a great time on the south coast and were inducted directly into the English village pub life. Rich got up and sang and wailed harmonica with the local band, greatly impressing Mike Leadbitter and his friends. The conversation all weekend was, of course, about the who, what and where of the music we all loved officially cementing the beginning of Richard Newell, Blues collector and musicologist. It became his true, life-long passion, possibly even more important to him than playing the music live himself.

These people were dedicated to finding out more about the recording artists, the studios, the cities that they played and recorded in. For them it was not enough to collect the records. They started making field trips to America to interview forgotten recording artists from the '40s and '50s, scoping out cities and regions like Memphis, New Orleans and South Side Chicago where the music had developed They tried to find the record companies that made these awesome records and, of course, to buy as many records as possible. Mike Leadbitter and John Broven went on to write books about the Blues putting together lists of labels, who recorded what and when and with whom, complete with the record numbers, etc. Rich supplied many valuable pieces of information in those early days culled from his always expanding record collection and growing contacts with other North American and European collectors and DJs.

> I was introduced to barley wine that weekend
> Help!
> then it was time to hook up with the rest of the band

When the time came to meet the rest of the band and Peter Rood, Richard and I took the train from Victoria Station, London to the coast and across the North Sea to Amsterdam by ferry. Let me moan right here about the number of people they pack onto those cross-channel ferries and this was back in '65! The middle of summer and grillions of Brits off on Cliff Richards-style continental holidays and the continentals goin' over and coming back from swingin' London, maybe a Japanese subway stuffer could pack a couple more bodies aboard but I seriously doubt it. Barely enough space to boogie and then that old wave-action begins.

well

enough

Downtown Amsterdam late at night and just off the ferry and straight away something going on everywhere. Dead tired from drinking all day on the ferry we managed to find a funky hotel on a canal in the old section of Amsterdam where we landed and spent the night. Next day we took a walking tour of the area. Awesome. Canals. Old, old buildings. History. History. History. Soon it was time to show up at a dock eight miles outside Amsterdam so we hailed a taxi, told the driver the name of the place the boat was docking with the rest of the band and zoom off we went.

He left us sitting in the middle of a field. A fuckin' field 8 miles from downtown Amsterdam. Nothing but space and the taxi gone and man, this can't be right. This can't be it. Did we get the lingo wrong? Did he not understand where we wanted to go? Or did he just rip us off, dump these Canuck hicks in the nearest field, grab the fare and then back for the next sucker? Eight miles from fuckin' nowhere when up steams this boat to, hey yeah, there *is* a dock here, water at the edge of the field anyway, and there's suddenly a flurry of activity, men bustling out of this little shed we'd hardly noticed. The boat gets closer and closer and there. Right up at the very front. In the prow! The balance of the Good'uns. Lookin' like a bunch of pirates. Yellin'. And hootin'. And wavin'. And then here come the guys tumbling down the gangplank.

Up to a fence surrounding the docking area and over the fence comes the big trunk containing all the records we'd arranged for them to bring over. And over came the guitars too! After all who wants to fuck around in customs tryin' to explain in Double Dutch why in the hell we're bringin' in a couple of thousand used records into the country without a permit and no we are not going to resell them and no we're not illegally importing American guitars

for profit and no again we're definitely not a Rock'n'Roll band come to play in the country
thereby working illegally.

So

    if you're not then where's your work visas?

and

    oh you don't have one eh!
    then we better bar you from our country
    Sorry boys!
 Why bother eh!
 too much hassle
 Much easier the over-the-fence way
 but don't try that in the 21st century
 ouch!

And there was Peter Rood driving up in his VW van. Good god we were trusting!

Peter Rood drove officially into our lives. Peter the Rabbit. The Playboy Rood. Walked
like a penguin. Talked like a penguin. Looked like a penguin. A penguin with a carrot top.
Pumpkinhead in black leather. With a white disposable aquafilter hangin' off his lips as he
enjoyed his Marlboro's.

 livin' in Germany
 dealin' in sin
 of many kinds

We suspected him, as we got to know him, of anything. An expatriate American from Los
Angeles. Probably a fugitive. Possibly an army deserter before it was fashionable. And
anyway who'd desert when stationed in Germany with Viet Nam as the alternative, unless
you've really fucked up.

 but we didn't know that then
 and can only guess at most of it now
 a speedin' pill popper
 a real gone topper!

We stopped and got some Wimpy burgers and beer and headed out for the Netherlands/West German border. Rood told us to get our passports ready and keep our mouths shut at the border. Let him do all the talkin'. That we would tell them we were just cuttin' through West Germany on our way to play a gig at the Tivoli Gardens in downtown Copenhagen and everything would be cool.

What the...?

We got through OK and eventually got to The Copa Cabana Club where we would be staying initially. This was Rood's home base where he had his special Playboy Rabbit-logo laden bedroom. No sooner there it was stop by Rood's room and check all this out! Almost went blind the precise moment I stepped across the threshold. Black light. My first experience. And fluorescent, soon to be psychedelic, paints everywhere. Black light soon to be blinding me in every club I was to visit in Germany. Soon to sweep the bedrooms of the world! Look out! A fuckin' phosphorescent mural of an A-TOMIC bomb exploding in the desert and rising from the head of his bed of white silk sheets glowing insanely in the black light. Peter Rood: Playboy International Rabbit #1.

Our beds? *This ain't North America!* The beds were pretty weird, no sheets, just a big fat feather filled comforter on a solid platform in a big, nothing else in it, room and then there were the TOILETS. You wanna' take a crap, put your feet into the imprints sunk into the tiles either side of a hole in the floor. GO! The first night I couldn't sleep much but at dawn, which came at about 3:30 a.m. I heard a great whoosh outside and I looked out our room window and there flying by was a giant, deep-yellow, hot-air balloon. *Check that out first time out of The Hammer dudes, wow, we're really out there, over here, this ain't too bad, I think I can live with this. What else new is there to see out there?*

And the ancient Copa Cabana Club featuring the internationally unknown "American Bar." Whoever went there? The whole three days we were there it was desolation row, except for us, Rood and the staff. Most of the main floor of this dump was a 1,500 seat dining and dance hall. Must have been the cat's longjohns back in, say, 1939. Things perked up for a few minutes the third day when one of Rood's other bands rolled in from England. Dig it!

B-Girl and The Vice-Squad. Showed up to play a set for some prospective local club owners. Shake it baby all night long. Seems B-Girl and her band were real money-makers. Definitely a somewhat different sensibility going on over here.

The next day after he got over the shock that we had instruments but no amps, Rood took us to some music shop he had a line of credit with or something to black mail them with and had us set up with the rest of the equipment we needed. We hadn't brought our amps or drums or sound system as they were way too awkward and expensive to ship. But Rood's shop had no up to date American stuff. Just junk. An Echolette guitar amp that looked great but only had a shitty little hi-fi set speaker in a cabinet big enough for twin 18's, for example. Richard did find a Hohner Accordion amp that turned out to be pretty good for harmonica.

Outfitted we were back to the Copa for food and beer and then off to the nearby Kon-Tiki Klub to see another one of Rood's associate bands. Some Indonesian group from Holland that wore shiny suits and Elvis hair and cloned pop hits from the past and present. The club was decorated to look like the inside of a raft. Go figure eh! Fishnets and baskets and wood panelling everywhere. And the inevitable red and white check tablecloths. We watched the band for about an hour. Not to our taste and then we got up and did a set only to find out we were sadly out of shape after not playing together for six weeks. Enough of this shit. Back to the Copa and an all night rehearsal.

We were there for three more days and played every night but It turned out there was no audience at the Copa except for the regional club owners Rood was trying to interest in booking us, dropping by to check us out. It was okay. We needed time to get used to the new equipment and get back in shape. Rood's plan was to book us into small clubs situated close to American and Canadian army bases where the German owners hoped to draw the soldiers in to spend their pay listening to back-home type music.

Booking us close to North American occupation troop military bases proved to be a clever move. Word soon got around about the new "American" group called The Good'uns. Rood had booked us into the Hill Billy Bar on *Kaiserstrasse* in *Kitzingen-am-Main* close to an

Club Kon Tiki logo

American Army base where we played to enthusiastic audiences. We were especially popular with the black G.I.s, some of whom it turned out would drive over a hundred miles to the bar to hear us play.

Most of the soldiers we ran into were very happy to be in Germany instead of Viet Nam and we had a ball for a couple of months even though we were playing from 6pm to 2am most weekends. Sam the Sham had the #1 jukebox hit in Germany that summer with "Wooly Bully" and Dylan's "Subterranean Homesick Blues" was on the jukeboxes too. We added some recent Motown hits to our repertoire: "I Can't Help Myself" by The Four Tops, Marvin Gaye's "Hitchhike" and "Pride & Joy"; and of course Barrett Strong's "Money," which was a huge Detroit fave even before the Beatles cover.

The club itself was small, a low, one-storey bunker with a gravel parking lot on the edge of town. A bar ran down the right side. The stage was in the middle at the back with a small dance floor down front. The balance of the room filled with tables and chairs. No frills if you don't count the large quantity of German *frauleins* decorating the joint which it turned out, were genuine B-Girls, as all the soldiers called them, who earned commissions from the bar owner for getting the soldiers to buy them shitty, fake, German cognac at inflated prices and more and more booze for the soldiers themselves, in the hope, I guess, that the soldiers might get to buy whatever else the girls might have for sale or take them to America. Everybody knew what was going on, but it didn't slow them down any. The soldiers were usually falling-down shit-faced before they had an opportunity to get anything up. The girls appeared to be very suicidal and many displayed slashed wrists and arms that were the result of over and over broken promises to take them back to the States and marry them. My man done left me Blues.

We were befriended by this cat from Chicago who seemed to be top dog with the black guys that frequented the club, called himself "Deadeye" and knew all the music we loved. We found him hangin' out on the *Kaiserstrasse* one night after our gig had ended and he claimed to be friends with Jr. Wells. It was early in the morning when he heard the Blues tunes we were playing, as was our wont before retiring for the day, on the portable record player we had with us and kept sitting in front of the open window of our ground-floor room. Deadeye comes breezin' over to the window and invites himself in. We chatted about the music for an hour or so and from then on at the Hill Billy we were between-set guests at his table where he introduced us to everybody he knew and man he was there every night and knew damn near everybody. He insisted on taking us back to his army base to feed us "real" food i.e. hamburgers, french fries, fried chicken and, well, bourbon if you count whiskey, as some of us do, as an important food group. And some nights, five cent beer, viva Michelob, plus el-cheapo American smokes which were very, very expensive in Europe at that time and which we all loved but didn't want to spend the excessive money on so we went with those dark Turkish tobacco German cigs, strong as all get out. Take me out to the canteen!

There were white guys at the club too, diggin' the grooves and jivin' with the chicks and in the beginning the balance was about 50/50. But the word got out and soon the blacks were outnumbering the whites 3 to 1. We were selling the place out of beer nightly but the owner was getting' scared and we heard he didn't like Afro-Americans to start with which I guess is why he called his joint the Hill Billy. The more that came, the more booze he sold, the more scared he got. Of course one night things got so wild and drunk and disorderly and inbred American prejudices sprung to the fore and an immense brawl broke out with Deadeye in the middle of it. The owner called the Military Police who arrived red lights flashing, sirens screaming, batons out and swingin'. I'm still on stage and suddenly Deadeye is beside me and sez' take care of this and drops his straight razor in my pocket and then makes himself scarce.

I just about shit myself. What if I'm searched by the M.P.s? A minute later someone else starts yelling at us to get out of the club "now," the owner is coming for the band and he's brandishing a pistol. I know he wants to shoot me because during all this we wouldn't stop playing 'cause it was way more fun to musically accompany the action, especially after 5 hours of straight playin' with exactly timed 15 minute intermissions. But now with gun play potentially added to the rhythm section it was grab the instruments and out the door. Pronto! That was it for the Hill Billy Bar. The owner kicked us out. After much hassle Rood made the owner pay up what was owed and on to the next gig.

> *too successful*
> *for our own good*
> *can't recall what happened*
> *to that straight razor*

Another wild place we played was the Copa. Yeah another Copa, sans "Cabana" (why spend money on the bigger sign that "Cabana" would have involved) in Soest which was in the Canadian patrolled zone of Western Germany. When those Canucks found out we were from Canada too, we were toast of the town. The last band that had played the Copa, one of those aforementioned Indonesian pop bands out of the Netherlands (remember the colonialism of the Dutch East Indies) had been so hated that the audience had thrown the band and all their equipment right through the club's front window, which was immediately behind the stage. The audience then went on to destroy the interior of the bar. It had just

been rebuilt before we got there.
> *jeeezus*
> *where are we now?*
> *kicked outa one joint*
> *on the toe of a riot*
> *and into another on*
> *riot's heels*

But we were from Hamilton, Ontario and proud of it and soon it was hey man I'm from Canada and then it was hey man I'm from Vancouver and hey man I'm from Regina and Kirkland Lake eh! and on and on. Musically we had what they wanted. These guys just had to hear our versions of Ronnie Hawkins' "Hey Bo Diddley" and "Forty Days" and "Marylou" over and over again, every night, and they really liked our take on David Clayton Thomas' version of John Lee Hooker's "Boom, Boom, Boom, Boom, Gonna Shoot You Right Down" as well. Good thing we could wail or we might have been picking glass from our asses too! As it was they contented themselves with getting pissed and picking fights with each other when they couldn't find any of the other allied troops to beat on. A nightly extravaganza of booze, violence and rock. A highlight of this gig was the wood-crate two-fours of litre sized beers outside our bedroom door every morning. Rock On! The downside was the endless playing on the juke box all day all night of Sam the Sham and The Pharaohs' "Wooly Bully."

After the first few days Richard started going home every night with one of the waitresses. He wouldn't come home until dawn and then slept all day until it was time to go on stage again. Well, everybody needs some routine in life and if this was the discipline of the road it was fine by us but after a few days Richard didn't bother to dress up for the gig. He'd arrive to play the first set in his pyjama top instead of his suit jacket. This was his idea of showmanship. Look back at that pic of us in our seersucker suits. Now picture Richard in the middle wearing his pajama top buttoned over his T-shirt. The band couldn't stop laughing either.

When Rood turned up near the end of our time in Soest he asked us if we wanted to play in England because that was where we were going next. We thought he had got ambitious at last because that was where we wanted to be, as much fun as Deadeye and NATO troops could be. In fact, we were ecstatic. England had been our objective in the first place. The major stumbling block to Rood's plan, which we didn't find out until we were at British customs and it was too late, was that Rood himself had been banned from the British Isles sometime earlier.

> *Be cool guys*
> *and lie*
> *everything will be fine.*
> *we never learned why.*
> *probably something to do with*
> *concealing unwelcome substances*
> *or weapons.*
> *or whores.*

But some little thing like a government ban didn't stop Rood. He loaded us into his Volkswagen bus and off we went back to England disguised as tourists. Little did we suspect.

Back in London and cutting costs, Rood and Newell stayed with Richard's grandfather in the East End. Ron, Andy and Babe were set up in a one room bed-sit while I bunked in with relatives way out in Sidcup, Kent just at the end of city transit routes back then. I'll give him this: Rood hustled on our behalf pretty well. At first. Then one day, after a seemingly successful audition (we got a standing ovation from the numerous other bands auditioning that same day) at London's Marquee Club (made famous in the movie "Blow-Up") we returned to

...nothing.

COOL FOOL

Peter Rood and his mini-bus
    were gone
    up the pipe
    puff of smoke
    nowhere to be found
    where?
    why?
    and most important: Now what?

We called our record-collecting musicologist buddy Mike Leadbitter whom Richard had bonded with in Bexhill-On-The-Sea. Mike had some connections in the London recording and bookings scene. A few gigs were scraped together but they didn't pay much split between five guys and in the end we didn't have the monetary resources to hang around London much longer. It's super expensive now. It was super expensive back then. Same as it will always be for a major planetary crossroads urban centre.

A few days after Rood abandoned us (or perhaps been abducted by aliens) Babe and Andy said they were homesick, that they'd had enough and Bam! They returned to Canada. Rich, Ron and I attempted to find an English drummer as a replacement and stay on. Mike Leadbitter found us a pub to hold auditions in. After what seemed like an endless day and listening to dozens of drummers we couldn't find anyone that knew how to play that lean, clean **Willie Smith** shuffle swing-beat with the right whack on the snare of the two and the four that we had to have for our music to work. Richard couldn't take it. We cancelled the few remaining upcoming gigs and headed on home. At least we'd gotten over there and given it a go! Quite the learning experience at the age of twenty-one and it didn't dampen our appetites for playing the Blues any. I mean, it was about the commitment, remember? And now we could be billed as
    "fresh from their European tour!"

Walkin' By Myself (After England)

Back from England bent but not broken and inspired by what we'd seen and heard, in early 1966, Richard, myself, Ron Copple and Babe Myles tried to put something together along the lines of the new music we had heard in Europe, as in The Yardbirds, The Small Faces, The Sorrows and of course, the early Who. We started working toward writing our own material, learned some recent tunes we didn't mind like the Y'Bird's "For Your Love." Richard and I researched regional booking agencies and managed to get a prominent Toronto rep interested in the band. We travelled over to T.O. by bus, showed up at his house in Willowdale with a tape, photos and a line of jive about our European experiences. That got us a once a week, regular booking in Yorkville, which was becoming a creative musical hotspot.

Toronto Rythm&Blues cats had all been heavily influenced by the presence in the city of American singer/keyboard player Curley Bridges and his band The Crew. The other influence was trumpeter Frank Motley, a Crew member, both recording in Toronto in the late '50s, early '60s. By 1965 and 1966 Rythm&Blues-oriented groups accounted for more than half of the bar bands in Toronto and in the hipper bars in Ontario's bigger cities: Dianne Brooks, Eric Mercury, David Clayton-Thomas and The Shays, Jack Hardin and The Silhouettes, Shawne and Jay Jackson, The Majestics, Jon and Lee and the Checkmates, Richie Knight and The Mid-Knights, Bobby Kris and The Imperials, Roy Kenner and The Associates, The Five Rogues, later the Mandala with Domenic Troiano, Motherlode, Tobi

Lark, Jackie Shane. All these bands and singers and musicians came to Hamilton and played the high school dances, the dancehalls and the licensed clubs and The Downstairs. Either with their own bands or as a member of Hawkins' sex, drugs and Rock'n'Roll Hawks.

But on the other hand the music was changing yet again. "Subterranean Homesick Blues," the single, was a jukebox and pirate radio super hit in the summer of 1965 all over Britain and Europe. Hate it or love it a revolution in Folk Music was underway.

> *the air was ELECTRIC*
> *go Bob*
> *I'm leavin' The Hammer*
> *I'm Yorkville bound*

In 1965 another Hamilton Mountain musician, drummer Ronn (Skip) Prokop, moved to Toronto and formed a Rock band The Spats. In 1966, with the addition of singer-songwriter and 12-string guitarist Adam Mitchell, the band was renamed The Paupers and emerged from the Yorkville coffeehouse scene with two dissimilar styles then new to Canada: Folk Rock and Psychedelic Rock. Though short-lived, The Paupers were one of the most progressive and musically talented Canadian rock bands of their day. After their demise in 1968, Prokop became co-leader of the very successful Lighthouse, a rock orchestra, formed in 1969 by Skip and the keyboardist-vibraphonist Paul Hoffert. Organized as a 13-piece band, Lighthouse made its debut 14 May 1969 at the Rock Pile (Masonic Temple) in Toronto.

> *yes! yes!*
> *get me to Yorkville!*

A band that influenced us because they came to Hamilton a number of times, playing the Teen Town Club above Arliss Shoe Store downtown on King Street East was Jack London and The Sparrow. Formed in 1964 they grooved a very progressive Blues-oriented music. By 1965 the band comprised of John Kay, at that time a Yorkville (there's that word again) coffeehouse regular, on vocals, harmonica and guitar, Dennis Edmonton, guitar, Goldy McJohn, organ and piano, had turned into Steppenwolf whose monster hit tune "Born To Be Wild" still resonates today. And there was The Ugly Ducklings. Formed in Yorkville Village in 1965 they became a driving force in getting the area noticed based on their Rolling Stones-inspired "bad boy" reputation. In 1966 they released their first single, "Nothin," on the Yorkville label and followed that with several more singles concluding with the chart topping "Gaslight" in 1967. And hey-Sue! Don't get me started on those Yorkville darlings Rick James and the Mynah-Birds.

Wow! Sounds like the creative way to go. Fuck the bar scene. And we had to bypass the Toronto Rythm&Blues guys or what?

> *hey, this a-way*
> *singers, songwriters*
> *do your own stuff?*
> *yeah!*
> *death to the bar bands!*
> *pop-icon me!*

After the arrival of BritRock in North America, '63-65, it became acutely apparent that the bar band circuit that so many of my contemporaries believed was the way to success in music, was an alternative way to earn a living and much more fun than sweating it out in an office or factory *but* B-Band participation was *not* the way to recording success and eventual stardom. B-Bands were useful for getting your shit together but at some point you had to break away from the front-man-and-hired-help concept of the bar bands

scene after SCENE
theatre - coffeehouse
14 VICTORIA AVE. N.
HAMILTON, ONT.
529-9270

24.

Doug Carter
the above named is
a contributing member
in the year 1971
validating signature
date Jan. 22, 1971

After-hours clubs such as Scene after Scene were an important part of Hamilton's creative music scene extending into the '70s.

and the bar owners' give-them-what-they-already-know mentality. You had to put together a "tru" group, a musical collective. Everyone equally responsible and co-creating new, original music. The best North American example I can think of is The Band. Song writing was hot! Groups were hot! All you had to do was listen around you. People in the music biz were doing exactly that. Ray Davies. Bob Dylan. Songwriting teams were hotter: Lennon and McCartney, The Glimmer Twins, to name just a couple. By '67 this shift had taken over the music biz in a big way, eventually begetting the sing/songwriter/guitar gunslinger. Move over and let Jimmi take over.

To try and sound progressive we had decided to call ourselves Young Fashion Ways after a tune by Muddy Waters. It sounded perfect for the musical market emerging and later on a possible clothing and perfume line. Yeah, it's only my bad luck you're not smelling like "Doug" right now. Anyway, after months of rehearsal and just a few weeks of exposure to the Toronto market Richard was snatched up by The Mid-Knights, a Toronto retro Rock'n'Roll/Rythm'n'Blues band, replacing the lead singer Richie Knight who, during the summer of 1963, had had a hit record on the leading eastern Canadian radio station of the time, 1050 CHUM-AM, with "Charlena." It was a huge Ontario hit. The single went on to sell in excess of 100,000 units (platinum in Canada). Every dance wanted the band because, with a hit record, the teens flocked to wherever the band played. Richie Knight and The Mid-Knights played virtually every major dance hall in Southern Ontario. The Balmy Beach Canoe Club. Crang Plaza. The Met. Mazaryk Hall. The Jubilee Pavilion in Oshawa. The Pav in Orillia. Then on April 25, 1965 Richie Knight and The Mid-Knights would return to Toronto and Maple Leaf Gardens as opening act for The Rolling Stones.

After Knight left the band to pursue a solo career or whatever and there were still a lot of gigs out there at Ontario high schools for the "Charlena Band" and possibilities of more recordings and that was that! Give me the money honey! One single was recorded by Richard with the Mid-Knights, a cover of Sam & Dave's "Soul Man," for Warner Brothers.

As for me, well, somebody done changed the locks on my door. Coming back from England was not peaches and cream. Before I knew it I was booted out of my basement snug in the parents house and onto the streets. On my own from now on. Hey, I was 22 eh? Time to make my own way in the world. I'd been over 'ome, seen the world after all. Europe anyway.

The first few days were rough as I didn't have much of the essential: cash! Some cat I knew from the bars and coffeehouses put me up on a couch till I could find my feet.

> down to the employment office
> down to the welfare
> down to a string of warehouse and
> office clerk jobs lasting between
>   one and six months
> or for as long as I could stand it
> or until I had enough weeks in to
>   collect the UI benefit
> down to always looking for a way
>   to play music for a living again

Out of work, out of money, only a radio for entertainment and bubblegum music dominating the charts, living in a mousehole attic on Jackson Street West where I owed back rent. One day, out of the blue, former Bishop drummer Ron Knappett knocked on my door with an offer. Along with singer Pat Sullivan and guitarist Dave Burt he was putting a Contemporary Rock band together and they desperately needed a bass to get the group up off the ground. And they were working on their own tunes. The offer: Ron would let me stay at his place in Burlington.

" *The Incredible Son's of Dr. Funk* "

JOHN FARR
Manager

HAMILTON

Telephone
416-522-6251

The Incredible Sons of Dr. Funk
From left: David Burt, Ron Knappett, Pat Sullivan, Doug Carter

late night
we moved my stuff
whew!
keep on rockin' don't look back

More about that later. What I'd been trying to do, before Knappett knocked on my door, was advance musically from the Blues. (I originally wrote "progress" musically from the Blues, but on second thought, shifting away from the Blues is not progress.) The more styles you could play, the more opportunities you had to play. I had choices. There was the coffeehouse scene and the disco scene. Yeah, there was disco before there was "Disco," the pop music craze fuelled by the discovery of the fuckin' get-on-my-nerves repetitious bloody drum machine. Lord give me strength. But back in 1966 bars were following the Whiskey A-Go-Go idea to become "discoteques" and the beginnings of Funk were beginning to show up in The Hammer too. Wicked Wicked Wilson Pickett was HOT!

waitin' at midnight for that "Mustang Sally"
where is that woman?
try dialing "634-5789"

I tried out for this band that was being put together by Russ McAllister, who was already an old warhorse on the local music scene, having been playing and singing since the very early '60s in The Vermonts. He did a very passable Johnny Rivers and Roy Orbison, if you were into that stuff, but he wanted to go Rythm'n'Blues. The Blues may be cool, but R&B was hot and you gotta' give the people what they want. I lent him a slew of records of that genre to study on and we got down to doin' it. Bobby Shaw was on B3 organ which lent the whole affair Funk authenticity. But no horn section. Not many bands around town tryin' to play this new groove, other than Bobby Washington's Soul Society, could afford a three-piece horn section. We did a number of gigs around town, but one night on our way to one of our regulars at some union hall on the second floor of a non-descript brick building on Parkdale North, me ridin' with Russ after helping load the equipment in the trailer he was pulling, and we went through the intersection at Wentworth and Main East.

and heard the big bang

lemme tell you
it was more than a theory
We turned, looked through the back window and
holy shit!
the trailer was gone
all the equipment
the bass
the amps
the speakers
the B#
were strewn across Main Street
guess that band's done gone
what can I get into next?

Maybe the discoteque scene. Discos
in the mid '60s were usually hole-in-
the-wall joints: big rooms upstairs over
old retail stores in the degenerating
downtown core, or scary-oh, hope-
there's-no-rats-in-here basements.
Non-alcoholic. BYOB. They competed
with the coffeehouses for the same
sort of cheap, do-what-you-need-to-do
ambiance, but more of a Rock edge.
Back in those days, every week there
was an ad in The Spectator classifieds:

Harrison Kennedy and
The Master Hand, 1967

Bass Player Wanted. I answered many of those adverts lookin' for a groove, one that turned
out to be a singing drummer from the West Mountain who had a regular gig lined up at some
upstairs disco on John Street North between King and King William. The idea was to play
Contemporary Pop music that teens would want to dance to. Get 'em to buy a membership,
drink the watered down cola, meet the opposite sex with interests similar to their own and

without adult supervision. I learned a lot of Beatles, Billy J. Kramer, Searchers, etc. Like the Liverpool Sound man! For all I can remember the joint was maybe called the Upstairs Cavern. That tanked too. Nobody came. Ferry Cross the Mersey have mercy! Next?

I wasn't much into the Folk Music/coffeehouse scene and didn't participate in it musically. After all, they were the anti-electric Ludites, but once in a while some old acoustic Blues guys showed up in town (emphasis on "acoustic") and one time it was a real treat: Yank Rachell and Sleepy John Estes playing upstairs in the old Federal Building beside the John Street post office. Way cool. But that joint didn't last too long either. Too many effin' stairs.

Around the same time, 1966, that other Hammer Blues/R&B band, The Bishops, broke up as well. Russell Carter and Harrison Kennedy formed The Master Hand with Russell's younger brother Larry Carter on drums, Bob Stewart on sax and Jim DeCecca on bass. Bishop's bassist Bobby Washington formed The Soul Society, one of the first and best of the Hamilton Soul bands featuring a three horn line.

In March 1966 The Spectator cited the explosion of bands in the Hamilton area, including The Roots of All Evil, The Rising Sons, The Reefers, The Pharoahs, The Seven Shillings, The XLs, The Plymouth Rockers, The Castels, The Marquis, The Plaques,The Sounds of Silence, The Penetrations, The 007, The Coachmen, The Keynotes, PJ and The Viscounts, The Misfit Six, The Phynx, The Shires, The Torpedoes, The Auroras, The Shades, The Sleepers, The Yorkshires, The Jesters, The Ancients and The "In" Crowd. We called them all The Plenthora. According to long-established band leader Jimmy Begg, secretary-treasurer of the Hamilton Musicians' Guild, there were as many as 25 rock bands earning money on local circuits.

As for me, this was the only time I did hit the road on the bar circuit, via the aforementioned Harold Kudletts. 1966 and I was desperate for money. For work. For a place to stay. Rick Golka told me the band he was in needed a bass player and suggested I come meet Louis Curtis. Probably the low point of my Blues career ambitions. On the road we went, myself, Rick, Ken Coombs on drums and two long-legged dancers: The Louie Curtis Revue. Louis sang in heavily accented English.

'ello Dolly

      eh wot?

The girls danced to show tunes like,

      wait for it

      "The Can-Can"

      no, we can't

      but I had no choice

First stop was Kirland Lake! Then down the road to Rouyn-Noranda. Followed by North Bay, and, finally, the bright lights of Sudbury. When we eventually landed at Hamilton's Grange Tavern I waited out the gig and split. Enough of that 6-nights-and-a-matinee, on-the-road-in-the-Canadian-wilderness shit.

By 1967 Ron Copple had joined Bobby Hebert, bass, a friend of ours, Mike Oddie, vocals and harmonica and Larry Carter who had recently left the The Master Hand to play in The Jameson Roberts Revolution which featured Russ Weil on the Hammond B3. Weil had been playing sax and piano with Bobby Curtola. During his later career teaching music for the Hamilton Board of Ed. Weil formed the perennial student All Star Jazz Bands and now has "Dr." fronting his name. Hebert and friends used to come around

Jameson Roberts Revolution. From left: Bob Hebert, Bob Pushing, Russ Weil, Larry Carter, Ron Copple and Mike Oddie

*Ronnie Hawkins, Richard Newell and Jay Smith about 1970
at Le Coq D'Or, Yonge Street, Toronto.*

and watch The Chessmen practice at the chip store on Brucedale by East 13th Street. Ron and I gave them some of their early music lessons. Musically the Revolution fell somewhere between R&B and early Psychedelic Rock. It was around this time too when Harrison Kennedy went off to Detroit to recording success as a key component of Chairmen of the Board.

Richard was the Mid-Knights' "Richie" for only a short while. Ronnie Hawkins was playing a week-long booking with one of his post-The Band Hawks at The Grange Tavern on King Street West. Ron Knappett and I went down to see them and I got to talking with Hawks keyboard player Richard Bell during one of the breaks. I knew Bell slightly from travelling down to Toronto occasionally with Richard Newell when he went to his Mid-Knights gigs in which, at that time, Bell had been a member. When Bell asked if I knew where Richard was these days I said most days he was home up on East 25th St. Bell called Ronnie Hawkins over and Ronnie asked me to get hold of Richard and see if he would come down to audition for the Hawks at the Grange the next night. I called Richard the next day and we both went down that night. Ronnie called Rich up to the stage to sit in. After Rich sang and played his harp Ronnie called out to the audience, "That boy reminds me of the King Biscuit Flour Hour on the radio station that I used to listen to back home," which was a live, noon-hour radio broadcast out of Helena, Arkansas, hosted for years by Sonny Boy Williamson II and featuring assorted guests. "That young man is so good on the harmonica, he is the 'King Biscuit Boy'," Ronnie told the audience and that was it. The Biscuit was born!

And Richard had a new gig. He joined Ronnie's band, a version of the Hawks that eventually featured Richard, Jay Smith, formerly of The Majestics (I'd seen them a couple of times especially at The Downstairs) and the awesome female vocalist Jackie Gabriel. What a front line of vocalists.

Meanwhile, what was I doing' hanging out with former Bishop's drummer Ron Knappett? It was early 1967 when I hooked up with Ron, along with Dave Burt, guitar, who came from an early Hammer proto-psychedelic band The Roots of All Evil and Pat Sullivan on vocals and rhythm guitar. Together we were The Incredible Sons of Dr. Funk. Bring on the sequins, the mauves and oranges, the boots and flares, the paisleys, the psychedelics. We were ready, playing stuff like
> Van Morrison's "Brown Eyed Girl"
> Alvin Robinson's "Something You Got" &
> Larry Williams' & Johnny 'Guitar' Watson's vocal of
> Cannonball Aderly's Jazz hit "Mercy, Mercy"

That last one was the same tune The Buckinghams scored a weak-kneed pop chart hit with, but it helped carry the Sons to a gig at The Downstairs in its dying days.

After several months of inadequate work the Sons hooked up with Fraser Loveman out of St. Catharines who had just left the very successful early Brit-Rock styled band The British Modbeats who, already aware of the British turmoil before it ever made it to American shores in late '64, early '65, were quick to capitalize on the craze and were the first to wear paisley, bell bottoms and shaggy hair, driving Ontario teens out of their bopper minds (and parents too but for totally different reasons.) After creative differences with the Modbeats, Loveman needed a band. What he had was that rare thing for a Canadian at that time: records out on a Canadian record label, Red Leaf

Records. We became The Fraser Loveman Group and besides the paisley etc. were soon featuring Canada's first liquid light show, the idea freshly imported from the 'Frisco Filmore by the St. Kitts' chapter president of the Satan's Choice outlaw biker gang who had taken a liking to Fraser. The cat was also considerate enough to provide some weed to go along with the groovy visuals. Wow! This was the first time I'd seen maryjane, smoke, pot, nickel bags (remember those?) joints. Only read about this shit. Until now. *Well let's fire up and see what all the fuss is about! I just want to talk about the room behind my—huh!*

> *gone, gone, gone*
> *up, up and away*
> *and the Blues was on hold*

We played a real eclectic mix of music styles: Sam and Dave alongside Big Brother and The Holding Company, Vanilla Fudge riffing on The Supremes ("You Keep Me Hangin' On"), Jimi Hendrix's "Purple Haze," Dave aced that guitar sound, and also stuff like The Doors' "People Are Strange" and much more along that line. Psychedelic and Soul music were here. Dammit, the music's changing again, man, time to get a sex machine or a psychedelic shack or some other damn thing! John Ord played B3 organ and Mike Gorgichuk was on rhythm guitar. Ron wired up his twin bass drum pedals with contact switches and put light bulbs in each. They'd flash with each bass beat Ron laid down on either drum. Wow, was he ever plugged in! The bass-beat flicker mixed great with the black lights and the liquid light stuff and lysergic acid or wheat rust or whatever it was Tom was raving about in "Gravity's Rainbow" and that the high school kids we played for were most likely on. If it wasn't weed and/or lots of alcohol and nicotine. Fraser was a great showman and the band commanded top dollar for its time. Loveman had a contingent of female followers who created costumes for him and the band, especially skin-tight bell bottoms, which we supplemented with military jackets, caftans, scarves and beads, very hippy dippy. And of course we grew our hair long and tried out not shaving to see if we could do beards.

DEBUT

FRASER former singer with the Mod-Beats proudly introduces his new band "THE FRASER LOVEMAN GROUP," Friday, October 6th at the Hamilton East Kiwanis Boys Club. YOU JUST GOTTA BE THERE!

Above:
The Fraser Loveman Group,
Fraser, David Burt, Ron Knappett, Doug Carter
Pat Sulllivan (right front) and John Ord (left front).

Right:
FLG Advertisement for
Sgt. Pepper's Lonely Hearts Club
at the Castle in St Catharines, Ontario.

SGT. PEPPER'S LONELY HEARTS CLUB
AT
THE CASTLE
FRIDAY
THE
Fraser Loveman Group

SPECIAL NOTICE: Sgt. Pepper's Lonely Hearts Club is open to all teenagers — no memberships are necessary.

We rehearsed all summer in the basement of Fraser's parents home in St. Catharines.

Ron, Pat, Dave and I were living in a beat-out old farmhouse outside Fonthill owned by John Ord's father. Daytime we had nothing to do but smoke pot, play our instruments and try our hands at song-writing. All in all it was pretty cool. The FLG played clubs and dances all over Niagara and Hamilton. Lots of highs schools on our itinerary and we played the East End Kiwanis Club in The Hammer a number of times. It was a major, east-end dance at that time that featured live music. Fraser had a large and loyal following there, as he did at the Castle, his home base in St. Catharines. We worked

87

both clubs often. We even got out on the road around Ontario a little bit, making it as far as some now forgotten bar in the Byward Market area of Ottawa. But when a new record didn't emerge for Fraser the gigs became sporadic. New bands came along everyday it seemed, with records and airplay, and eventually everyone in FLG went off their separate ways.

Dave Burt went with Neil Merryweather to California, recording a couple of albums as Merryweather for Capitol Records. They received critical, if not commercial, success. After that, in 1971, Dave was an inaugural member of the multi-lingual musical cooperative CANO that went on to long success in Canada, especially in Francophone communities outside Quebec.

Ron became more and more involved in studying drums and turning himself into the Jazz drummer he was eventually to become, playing and recording with Danny Lanois in his early Grant Avenue Studio years. For many years Ron drummed with Hamilton's foremost Jazz pianist, Paul Benton.

Me? In 1968 I got married and tried to do the regular thing with a day job that lasted about a year before I started to look for another band to play in.

By the late '60s a plethora of bands had poured out of the basements and garages of our nation and their members weren't just the working-class youth desperate to avoid following their fathers' footsteps into wage slavery on industrial assembly lines. Middle and upper-class kids too were getting in on the act. You could tell because they were the ones with the really good equipment. Check out the line up on this poster from a circa 1968 "Battle of Bands" event held at Hamilton's Mohawk College:

Booker Fox
Buxton Kastle
Tranquility Base
Justin Bogsworth
Moll Flanders
Zingana
Old Sailor
An All Day Show
Featuring the finest in up and coming talent.
Doors open. 2p.m.
Admission $1.75
Saturday, April 17

Check out Buxton Kastle. Dig this Hammer pedigree history:

Gerry Doucette (aka J. Buxton) (lead vocalist)
Bob Johnston (Hammond B3, rhythm guitar)
Rick McIsaac (bass)
Russ McAllister (lead guitar)
David Kastle (electric piano)
Jack Pedlar (drums)

David Kastle had been in the The Mingels. Russ McAllister owned and managed a music store on King Street East and supplied some of their instruments when they put the group together in the late '60s. They recorded several singles, at least one engineered by a very young Daniel Lanois, for both RCA and then Reprise Records. The story goes that someone from Super K Productions spotted Doucette in a 1970 performance and took him stateside to record Bubble-Gum as The Kasenetz-Katz Super Cirkus. Buxton Kastle mutated into The Terra Nye Project before breaking up. Later, Jack Pedlar went Punk as part of Teenage Head and has had a very tasty solo recording career as well. He's also the premier Rock, or

Psychedelic Doug

anything that goes with it, Hammer drummer, still beatin' it out with the groove.

And then there's this local music history: Tranquillity Base.
 Ian Thomas, guitar and vocals
 Oliver McLeod, guitar and
   vocals
 Nora Hutchinson, vocals
 Bob Doidge, bass
 Nancy Ward, recorder and
   keyboards

In the mid '60s Ian Thomas formed the Dundas, Ontario, Folk trio Ian, Oliver and Nora, featuring Oliver McLeod and Nora Hutchinson. By the end of the '60s they were joined by Doidge and Ward and called themselves Tranquility Base. The band would record two singles for RCA "If You're Lookin," which went Top-30 in Canada, and "In the Rain," which didn't fare as well. The band was best remembered for their phenomenal vocal abilities and often performed with the Edmonton Symphony and the Hamilton Philharmonic. They split up in the early '70s after an album they recorded failed to impress RCA. Not too dusty for cats from the greater Hammer. My old friend Ron Knappett drummed for them near the end.

And somewhere back there in the early '60s was this very popular band, The Reefers, specializing in California suft songs a-la The Beach Boys and Jan & Dean, but nobody missed the wordplay in the band's name.

> *hey, give me one!*
> *hold that toke, oops*
> *I think I meant thought*
> *um, folks.*

Beginning in '67 with imported Mexican pot until '70 or so...when was Altamont?...next thing the Psychedelic Era was on! Bring on the LSD! Purple haze all in my what? I indulged a little bit in the name of scientific experimentation, you know, to find out what it was all about, but a 3-day acid trip scared fuck out of me. I was huggin trees before the green movement had hardly been invented yet. Thank the gods for the Whole Earth Catalogue and all the other eco-hippie shit. 'Shrooms and peyote were much more visually interesting, not so scary and not nearly so long lasting. But a lot harder to acquire than some other, more locally produced, products.

Messenger: standing Earl Johnson and Dave Klinko, sitting Keith Lindsay, Mike Oddie and Doug Carter

COOL FOOL

Some of my bandmates favoured booze with good uppers. LSD in the right quantity could keep you drinkin' and partyin' 'til the break of day. If you could get the prescription, diet pills dubbed "Black Beauties," did a wonderful job of keeping you functioning well into the party or through a gig at least, but it was an elusive acquisition. Lots of encapsulated fake speed was out there on the street. Maybe it was the real thing. Maybe it was rat poison. Some sort of meth also, if you knew who to talk to, and apparently we did.

Growing up on the East Mountain in the '50s and early '60s, most of the guys had mostly 3 choices: factory work, Rock'n'Roll, outlaw bikers. Behind door #3: lack leather jackets, greased-back hair, viscous smirks. *Oh! will he kill me now or wait for later?* Of course, we all knew each other to some extent and drank in the same taverns. *What can I do for you boys tonight, eh?*

Yeah, the East Mountain: Red Devils, Satan's Choice. Eventually the local hardcore turned into some of those guys far up the biker national foodchain where the club name has been copyrighted. Use it and get your ass sued.   *sued?*
     by a biker gang?
     sounds a bit "corporate," no?

And let's not forget the wannabes, the youngsters, the up and comers: the Outlaws. May be the guys you grew up with, but it's still crime and getting better organized all the time. Hey, we weren't all born Italian in The Hammer. One way or t'other, if you've got connections...
     meet me in the washroom
     the back alley
     show me the bread, man
     the bread
     and I'll let you have some product
     what you want
     what you need
     you're gonna fuckin' love it
     gonna rock all night
     with enough get up & go left over to work in the morning

92

believe it!
see ya tomorrow night.

With acquaintances like these it's not always easy to remember to keep the old connections, the ones who brought you to the dance.

Although we stayed in reasonably-close touch after his move to the Mid-Knights and on to the Hawkins band, I didn't get together with Richard again musically until the Christmas of 1970. It was at his parents' place on Coral Drive on the East Mountain. A bunch of us, friends new and old, got together for a jam session, intent on recording some old Chessmen tunes we were all fond of. In attendance, besides me and Richard, was drummer Vic Clement, a friend from our old pre-Chessmen days, drummer Babe Myles, guitarists Ron Copple and Earl Johnson and Paul Cronkwright sitting down to the Newell family piano. Earl was lead guitar in a band I was in at the time that featured Mike Oddie on vocals and harmonica. We called ourselves Messenger and played a lot of Joe Cocker, a little early Led Zeppelin with an assortment of Blues/Rock faves from the past and ongoing present.

Coral Drive was a festive get together of friends, old and new, and we wanted something to remember it by. We recorded:
Cookie & the Cupcakes' "Mathilda"
Muddy's "Tiger In Your Tank"
Chuck Berry's "Carol"
Smiley Lewis' "I Hear You Knockin' "
a couple of Excello tunes by Lonesome Sundown & Lazy Lester,
"Don't Go" & "You Know I Love You"
Little Walter's "Everything's Gonna' Be Alright" &
Little Richard's "Miss Ann"
And Mike Oddie provided a memorable vocal and harmonica solo
on Elmore James' "12 Year Old Boy"

To a small group of people, the "Coral Drive Sessions" became something along the lines of the "Big Pink" basement tapes legend, except that it was more a hallmark for the musical experiences of a particular time and place than the herald of a new sound. Still, this Xmas event would bear fruit.

Bobby Washington and the Soul Society: Bobby, Doug Risk, unknown trumpet, Jim Skarrat

Gotta Be A Good'un

So, yeah, I wake up one morning and it's like the fall of 1968, I'm married, somehow and living in a one room apartment on Concession Street and East 34th. That's one block from the house where I'd spent so many years growing up and trying to escape. Um, pass the coffee, gotta go to work.

work?
seems I've gone and got me a straight job
in the music biz?
sort of
um, wow, okay

I'm unloading 8-track tapes and cassettes from the backs of trucks, stacking them on shelves, unstacking them from shelves, selecting and packing them in cartons according to orders from various retail stores, filling out packing slips and putting the tapes and cassettes back on the backs of trucks to go to said various stores. I get this crazy job in the music biz because I am a musician and I know the pop music industry.

know who so and so is?
and so and so?
yeah?
you're hired

COOL FOOL

That's me, primo number one bass player since the dawn of history, or if not the dawn of history then the dawn of last Sunday at least, gigging for the Hamilton kings of the 8-track car stereo universe: The Muntz Music brothers.

Believe me, I was counting da muntz I worked there (rimshot please.)

But you remember 8-tracks. Cars wired up, for the first time, with sound coming out of all four corners of your auto-mo-beeel? A quick stop at our combo music store/installation location on King Street East between Sanford and Wentworth, south side, come Saturday night your little darlin' is totally squirmy with that big bass back-beat from Muntz' super-charged, thunka thunka, in-door speakers, running across her hips, down one long leg and up the other before heading straight to her heart!

> *oh baby yeah*
> *I feel it*
> *I feel it*
> *'course I love you*
> *I do*
> *I do*
> *you want it?*
> *I'll do it*
> *I'll do it*

And silence. Suddenly no more groovy vibes throbbing from Muntz' door speakers at all. What the . . . couldn't those sound jockeys in back of Muntz super installation station even connect a couple of wire's they've gone and left you flying solo man, just when you need them most but wait, no, you've only come to the end of the first "section" on the tape and there's like a minute or so you can't let your honey even think about re-hooking her bra strap and straightening out her skirt, until finally Jimi's back with that fabulous guitar solo or Annie finishes the bridge in that snowbird anthem thing or, what the hell, maybe that nun resumes dominiquing among the hills of Quebec because it's times like these, you know, we all got religion.

> *Oh god pulleeeez*

Well that lasted about a year and somehow it was take this job and shove it. Thank god the wife was working. Salvation, sort of, came forth in the shape of a phone call from Ron Knappett, he of the Bishops, the Incredible Sons of Dr. Funk, the Fraser Loveman Group and now with the newly formed Tractor created by saxophonist Jim Skarratt out of the remains of Bobby Washington's very successful for a time, Soul Society. Bobby had left and

they needed a bass player and they wanted to update their sound to what was hot in 1969. I may have been cooling my heels in the back rooms of the music biz for twelve months, but hey, I was still hot where it counted.

> *oh honey?*
> *I'm in a band again*

That lasted a few months before squabbling over money matters set in and the band broke away. We called ourselves Sundown and before I knew it me and the old lady were sharing living quarters with some other members of the band and their old ladies in a farmhouse out in the wilds of Binbrook. The Sundance Commune: Doug Risk, Chris Tootell, Jim Stewart, Bob Speakman, Ron Knappett. My hippy-dippy moment in time. There was music I'm pretty sure but mostly it was let's drop acid

Photo by **Gerry Laarakker**   **TRACTOR**   Jim Skarratt
525-5830
HAMILTON, Ontario.

Promo for Tractor, top: Doug Risk on guitar, Doug Carter with Risk,
Ron Knappett on drums,
middle: Ron, Jim Skarratt on sax,
bottom: Jim Stewart on sax, Bob Speakman on trumpet, Chris Tootell on keyboards

and conquer the world. The only thing I conquered after that . . . are you experienced? ...experience was my ... holy fuck what is happening to me? ... right now panic and fear. I came back down with my arms wrapped around a great big oak tree. The commune lasted about most of a winter, until the real sun came out to dance on Binbrook's golden fields and that damned oak tree let go of me. Lesson learned.

Back to the Hammer, an apartment downtown on Bold Street and I need another band or god forbid a day job. Thanks be I'm married to a woman with a steady job. What to do, what to do, I need money, that's a-what I want. Nobody wanted to play bass back then. It was all drums or flash lead guitar, first choice, if they didn't fancy themselves frontmen extraordinaire, but even clueless flash pluckers, bangers and vocalists usually knew enough to know they needed a solid bass behind their extraordinariness. So I answered one of the ads in the local rag *bass player wanted* and ended up commuting by bus to practice in the extreme east end out by the Red Hill Valley. Yeah, I'm talking way, way out there. Almost Stoney Creek. Well, it's all nice work if you can get it.

Below: Doug sings and plucks, Dave Klinko plays drums, with Messenger at Hamilton's Westmount High School circa 1970.

It was a vocalist, Bob Scott, a drummer named Doug Something and a guy name of Earl Ciszek, soon to be Earl Johnson in the Real Gooduns. A few months of gigs playing the Guess Who catalogue, stuff like that, it was again time to make a change. Playing music has got to be more exciting that this. Earl felt that way too. Goodbye Bob and Somebody Doug, hello Mike Oddie on Blues harp and vocals, Keith Lindsay on keyboards and Dave Klinko banging drums.

Oh yeah and we kept the name. Messenger was reborn. Rockin' Blues meet Leon Russell and Joe Cocker and fellow travellers.

For roughly the same two years Richard played with Hawkins. During that time Ronnie asked Richard to assemble a new version of the Hawks for him. Richard tapped hard-working Ontario bar band The New Ascots for Rheal Lanthier, guitar, Kelly Jay, keyboards and Roly Greenway, bass. As The Five Ascots they had a history of stuffing downtown Duffy's Tavern with hard-core rockin' Blues aficionados. Richard added existing Hawkins sideman, Richard Bell, keyboards, along with John Gibbard, guitar, and Larry Atamaniuk, drums, to create the latest version of Hawkins' band christened And Many Others. Hawkins took the band to some of the most prestigious venues in Rock including the Filmore East, opening for the likes of Joe Cocker, Johnny Winter and Mountain.

Ronnie Hawkins had a reputation as a hard taskmaster on the road. He was known for taking young, talented musicians living their local sex, drugs and Rock'n'Roll dreams and giving them the discipline to make a living in the business, which meant, mostly busting ass on the bar circuit. Officially drugs were a no-no, but two out of three ain't bad and I never knew many riders in the Blues bus to say "not tonight dear, I gotta drive to the Lakehead." But if you wanted to work for Ronnie you still had to get up and do the gig and there were plenty of pills around to get you on stage and alert enough to hold the beat. All you had to do to keep Ronnie's show on the road was not fuck up and not get caught. There were as many rumours about what "really" went on as there were people who might have known somebody who might ever have been backstage at a Hawkins show or said they did and had, but shit, you can for sure see Ronnie had his work cut out for him.

Like The Band, everyone left Ronnie eventually. In 1970, the backup crew that included Richard grew weary of hearing Hawkins describe them on stage, as "so dumb they could fuck up a crowbar." The boys still had a sense of humour and took the insult as their name of their new band, Crowbar, renting a big old farmhouse at the Hwy. 403 at the end of Mohawk Road in Hamilton. They called it Bad Manors and used it to live, rehearse and party in, telling Ronnie to go fuck himself. The act resumed with a slight personnel change: Sonnie Bernardi

Dave Klinko and Mike Oddie with Messenger at Westmount High.

replaced Atamaniuk on drums and Jozef Chirowski replaced Bell on keyboards. Crowbar came up with a record deal with Frank Davies' Daffodil Records. Along with Crowbar, Richard cut the *Official Music* album as the first Daffodil Records release in 1970 which went out under the name *King Biscuit Boy*. Crowbar also cut an album that contained the smash hit "Oh What A Feelin'."

So here's me and Messenger playing around the Golden Horseshoe, including twice at one of my favourite gig memories, the school for the deaf in Milton. They couldn't hear the musical subtleties but man they could feel the beat and weaved and bobbed and stamped their feet to the grooves and had a wonderful time. But my heart was still in playin' all the Blues all the time what with the horn bands patterned after David Clayton Thomas' Blood, Sweat and Tears and Skip Prokop's Lighthouse springing up everywhere. In The Hammer it was bands like the Brass Union, Vehicle and Young. (Remember the 45 "Grape Farm"? I didn't think so.) There just wasn't much opportunity or demand for the Blues on the local scene. Then in 1970, Richard, by now "Biscuit" to one and all, to everybody's surprise, suddenly left Crowbar.

Huh? Was he so dumb he'd fucked up Crowbar? Whatever, the move got me back with Richard. That was the year, during the Christmas holidays, of the jam at Richard's parents place on Coral Drive right around the corner from the home of future Canadian Blues guitar hero Jack De Keyser. Riding high on the success of Official Music, and with part two of his recording sessions with Crowbar about to be released as the album Gooduns, Richard looked to his roots in The Hammer and recruited myself on bass, Earl Johnson (who ended up with a great Blues teacher in Richard before eventually moving on to a semi-famous Canadian Rock group with at least one hit: Moxie) for guitar and Babe Myles, drums, to tour

Canada and the US and to record a new album for Paramount Records. Out of that Coral Drive jam came the rebirth of The Good'uns, adding Garnet Zimmerman on piano. Richard and I had used the name "Good'uns" in Europe back in 1965 when we found the continent already had an established band called The Chessmen, but this time the inspiration came from the title of Richard's second Daffodil release, "Gooduns" The new Gooduns (it was actually, formally The Real Gooduns) had another innovation: every night Richard played a half set of Elmore James tunes featuring himself on slide guitar. A wonderful, already vintage, sunburst Gibson Les Paul. Glass bottleneck. He sounded oh so Official.

That spring we put the band together out in Westdale, in the basement of fan, music lover and entrepreneur Michael O'Brien. It wasn't long after this that O'Brien and Michael Short went to work for Ronnie Hawkins' booking agency, upstairs at the Hawk's Toronto Coq D'Or Tavern on Yonge Street. Still later Michael followed his brother Martin Short to Hollywood as his main writer. He always claimed from the get-go that he'd taught Marty everything he knew and that was way before Marty became so famous. And O'Brien became a great band leader/ vocalist around The Hammer right through to the early '90s. He's the father of The Hammer's great, young rockin' pianist, Jesse O'Brien. And Richard still had a Toronto manager, a record contract with Paramount Records and a name that guaranteed gigs.

> *so we were gettin' out of The Hammer*
> *again*
> *at last*
> *again*
> *on with the show!*

Richard rehearsing in Michael O'Brien's basement in the spring of 1971.

Celebration Music, our managers, got a deal on the $100,000 sound system that had been assembled for the Toronto production of "Godspell." This is the show that linked young wannabe Hammerheads Martin Short, Eugene Levy and Dave Thomas with Andrea Martin, Gilda Radner and musical director/keyboardist Paul Shaffer, from which they all went on to things like Saturday Night Live, SCTV and professional television/movie careers. Also in the cast was Toronto's Jayne Eastwood, who had already appeared in Don Shebib's movie Goin' Down the Road and became a perennial CBC character actress, eventually moving to that part of Hamilton still known as Dundas.

> *droppin' all the names I can*
> *so you get it*
> *lots of hot Hammer talent*
> *goin down that road big time, all*
> *only three or four or five degrees shy*
> *when it came to the magical*
> *six degrees of separation*
> *from your's truly*
> *INSPIRATION!*

Godspell had recently moved into smaller digs at the Bayview Theatre and the sound system designed for the bigger Royal Alexandra was going beggin', but not for long. Or at least that's what the folks at Celebration told us. Band/management relationships were always uncertain, overlaid and undercut with paranoia. As a musician you just hoped that your manager worked as hard at getting you gigs as he did trying to convince you to remain his client. What's certain is that suddenly The Gooduns had the most awesome sound system of any band in Southern Ontario. Everything was miked and mixed through a large multi-track soundboard akin to that being used in the top recording studios of the day. The sound pushed by a massive amplifier system went out through stacks of speaker boxes on each side of the stage, each box designed to accommodate particular parts of the sound waves produced.

> *playin' the Blues*
> *LOOOOOOOOOOOOUUUUUUUUUUUUUUUUUUUDD!*

On the road we went to promote Richard's latest album. Showcase club dates around Toronto and Southern Ontario and high school gigs and high school gigs and more high school gigs. They paid bands big bucks back then. In early March we got what was, in retrospect, the most awesome gig that the band ever played: a full week at the number one Jazz and Blues club in Toronto, Yonge Street's Colonial Tavern. Dig it. The line up for the month of March was:

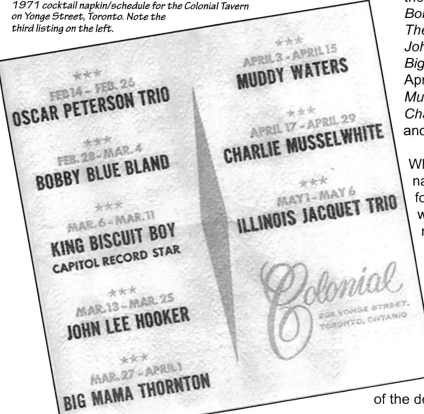

1971 cocktail napkin/schedule for the Colonial Tavern on Yonge Street, Toronto. Note the third listing on the left.

the Oscar Peterson Trio
Bobby 'Blue' Bland
The Gooduns
John Lee Hooker and
Big Mama Thornton
April followed with:
Muddy Waters
Charlie Musselwhite
and Illinois Jacquet

What a privilege to be among names like that. You might forgive us if we thought we'd arrived at Blues band nirvana.

Of course that meant we'd signed away our souls for the rest of our natural-born, creative lives to manger/agent/ financial advisor, Wayne (the Pear) Thomas of Celebration Music. Part of the deal with The Pear was that

we would record for Paramount Records.
>*Fine and dandy!*

They wanted mostly original material.
>*Fine and dandy (2)!*
>*Richard and I got busy*

We did what we could with the little recording equipment Rich had, but we needed demos to send off to the record company. Not much in the way of recording studios existed in The Hammer back then, but somebody told us about the Lanois brothers, Danny and **Bob**, who'd somehow come up with the cash to fulfill their passion to own a recording studio out in affluent Ancaster. Coincidentally, we'd recently been sampling a new, home-grown product known as Ancaster Green. Mmmm! Mmmm! Mmmm! Things just seemed to click right from the start.

The Lanois' first studio was set up in their parents' basement. That's where we ended up making our demos and they did a pretty decent job even with all the laundry tubs and washers and everything tucked back in the corners. Soon they had their own building and eventually the world famous Grant Avenue Studios was born. Danny of course went on to be one of, if not *the* premier record producer of his time and a very good singer/song-writer as well as sideman on various stringed instruments. I remember seeing him playing pedal steel guitar behind The Hammer's premier Folkie, Ray "Linda put the coffee on" Materick, at The Riverboat in Yorkville. By the way, we got the record deal! That's all that mattered back then.

But first, The Pear announced, he'd booked us to "tour" eastern Canada. In April! The first week! Spring might have been shyly poking it's head among the melting snow banks in Southern Ontario but up in Quebec and the other lord-thunderin'-jesus Maritime Provinces hangin' way out in the North Atlantic it was still friggin' nasty cold thank you very much. We eased ourselves back into winter with an overnight stop in downtown Quebec City drinking quart bottles of La Belle Province's corporate beers. Quart-size packaging was still not widely available in Ontario. It was 12oz-stubbies-or-nothin' at that time.

"Long neckers" had been standard packaging years earlier, but the shift to stubbie packaging was affected by the control major brewers had on the Ontario market. At a time when small regional brewers had all but died out and before neighbourhood micro-breweries began, Carling, Labatt, O'Keefe and the few remaining independents all used the same bottles, which meant no sorting returns in their conglomerate-owned Brewers' Retail stores, virtually the only shops where you could buy take-away suds back when. Very efficient and environmentally cool before that became a social-conscience issue, but man those squat, brown, neckless vessels were about as pretty as a midget wrestler. Quebec's quart bottles were novel to us, not to mention the extra beer they held. Left us in grand shape for the long drive through the endless woods of New Brunswick next day. On to Fredericton and St. John's and more high school gigs!

The Gooduns fooling around on the PEI ferry, April 1972.

Thank the gods I had a nice chunk of black hash to while away the miles. And then on to Nova Scotia and comin' in to Halifax, checkin' out all the Pop-Eye lookin' dudes lurching here and lumbering there. Elvis hair everywhere. We were in splints, falling out of the car laughing.

> *ahoy mates*
> *what do you do with a*
> *you know what etc.*

Don't ask me the name, but we did play a club gig in The Fax and then something in the town over the bridge, Doormouse or something, and then on to Prince Edward Island via the ferry for a gig at Summerside Arena. The hyacinths and tulips were popping up back in Ontario, but on the Island it was nothing but six foot snow drifts. We'd've called it "The Arctic

Circle Tour" except we didn't want to give The Pear ideas. The only colour we saw other than dirty white was from the candy wrappers and empty cigarette packs blooming from snow banks.

> *suddenly I got them*
> *deep in the maritime Blues*
> no wonder Hank Snow was bragging
> "I've been everywhere, man"
> yeah—everywhere *but here*

As antidote to the East Coast road life we checked out all the local beers. Wherever we went. No matter the weather. There might have been some quantity of rum involved as well. And maybe we were slipped a bottle or two of "screech" under the table. Fuck the weather!

But now, with the recording session coming up, it was suggested we might make positive use of our time (drinking apparently not considered "positive"—who knew?) writing some of our own songs. I came up with possible lyrics and structures for five songs and ran them by Richard, who revised the lyrics in places to suit his vocal style, or added a line or two to flesh out the story line, but his special talent was to suss the right sort of musical parts for everyone to play that would bring the song alive and keep it within the Blues mainstream. He knew how to make the sound official and could show each member of the band exactly what they needed to play if necessary.

Below: Cool Fool Doug doin' The Boogie Walk.

Back from the coast, we played a few more gigs around Toronto and Hamilton then, in early summer, we were in central Michigan playing gigs with Cub Koda and Brownsville Station who had come out of the Detroit proto-Punk Rock scene of the Stooges and the MC5 etc. Koda was a fantastic guitar player, showman and musicologist.

106

The band would hit the charts in 1973 with the Rock anthem "Smokin' in the Boys Room" which sold over two million copies and was covered by Motley Crue in the mid '80s. Then we were back to Toronto for a bit before heading down to Roanoke, Virginia (honey, where the green grass grows as Jimmy Reed sang) and Washington, DC. Most of these American gigs were at music festivals of one type or another in a variety of outdoor venues.

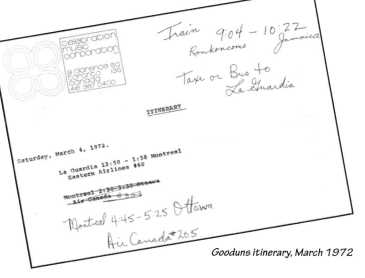

Gooduns itinerary, March 1972

Post concert one hot summer night after a gig in Roanoke we went back to the farmhouse of some musicians we'd met who were taken with the way we could play the Blues. It was way back up in the Virginia hills where we jammed and partied all night, the first and only time I got to try genuine moonshine.

> corn likker
> liver varnish
> white dog
> white lightning—whoooo!
> poured from a wide mouth
> mason jar
> and home-grown pot too
> Wowie Zowie!

We'd only gotten back into those wooded hills by following the tail lights of the other cars into the dead of night, yet somehow we managed to return to our motel at dawn. That remains a bit of a miracle to me still today.

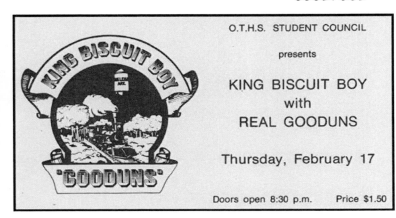

O.T.H.S. STUDENT COUNCIL

presents

KING BISCUIT BOY
with
REAL GOODUNS

Thursday, February 17

Doors open 8:30 p.m.   Price $1.50

High school dance admission ticket

And then Florida. Promise me a flight down to Miami Beach, a few days in one of those classic Art Deco beachfront hotels surrounded by retired New Yorkers and a booking into a ballpark-show opening for Mitch Ryder and The Detroit Wheels and I'll be waitin' on the curb for the airport limo every time. Mitch was just starting out to earn his second million, having lost the first he'd acquired with top ten hits such as the combo tune "Devil With A Blue Dress/Good Golly Miss Molly" via a variety of very bad habits. Next trip, fly me up to Ottawa for a gig at The Rainbow Bistro. It's not Miami but it's all work. You know, my kind of work: rockin' and rollin' Blues kind of work. And we still had the Gooduns album to promote.

Whenever and wherever we found spare time Richard and I continued to work on our original tunes for the upcoming recording session, rehearsing them with the rest of the band between gigs, then suddenly, before we knew it we were in New York City to record and also to play a Paramount Records showcase at Max's Kansas City! Oh baby that's a-what I like! Max's Kansas City was THE bar of choice for the likes of Andy Warhol, Lou Reed, and, like, take my breath away etc. etc. etc.

> *celebrities of many stripes &*
> *all that shit hanging out*
> *all the time*
> *like I said*
> *HOLY WOW!*

We bunked out on Long Island at some motel close to the Long Island Sound Recording

Studios that Paramount Records, in their infinite corporate wisdom, had chosen for us. This studio's claim to fame, we were told many, many times, was that it had recorded James Brown's mega-hit pop-crossover "It's A Man's World." They proudly gave us copies of their latest release: "Ain't No Greens In Harlem." No shit. Garbage men on strike, or something, whatever.

These were the days of the new, emerging, multi-track recording technology with early, miscellaneous electronic bells, whistles and gimmicks. The guys recording us were hooked on that shit. Richard preferred a more traditional sound. He bitched for it, but check out what they did to the mix of "Smoke Stack Lighting." Man, they did strange echo things with Richard's harp and electronically fucked with Earl's guitar leads on a number of tunes. We recorded the originals: "Blues for Duffy's Tavern," "Steel Town Blues (Wind and Rain)," "Deaf, Dumb, Crippled and Blind," "Gotta' Be A Goodun" and "Caledonia River." "Smokestack Lightning," if you ever get to hear this unreleased track, was a Howlin' Wolf cover. We also did the traditional Blues "Going To Kansas City" and Champion Jack Duprees' "Junkers Blues."

On the way back from NYC we stopped in Woodstock, New York to visit with Richard Bell, now of the Full Tilt Boogie Band, who Richard, The Biscuit, knew from as far back as his Mid-Knights days, and their guitarist, Stratford's John Till with whom Richard, The Biscuit, had also played in one of the many versions of Ronnie Hawkins' Hawks. Full Tilt Boogie had recently lost their leader and vocalist, Janice Joplin, whom they had backed up on her album Pearl. They were in Woodstock to record a post-Joplin album, trying to keep the great band alive. Ultimately it faded away but not before sharing a great night with us. Top it off, Paul Butterfield was also jammin' at a café bar in the middle of town and was that joint jumpin'.

Later that night I toked up with some rich black opium, my first and only such experience and it was amazing. We wandered around this town in the Mountains north-west of New York City marvelling at the universe and a sky filled with stars,
   wop bob a luba a wop bam…
   GONE!

SUMMER '71 Ottawa

Richard gives his head a spin in the nation's capital.

Boom, Boom, Out Go The Lights! The Long Island Sound album never got released. Surprise! Paramount Records, despite some success with its first signings like Commander Cody and The Lost Planet Airmen, turned out to be a shell company or something for a bigger media conglomerate and when accountants needed a tax write-off or something they just closed the label down. Whatever the reason, it happened just before the release of our album and that was the end of that. Within a few months the Gooduns were goners too.

Four of the five songs written by Richard and myself from that recording session have since been released on *Badly Bent: The Best of King Biscuit Boy*, Unidisc AGEK-2164. They are "Steel Town Blues (Wind & Rain)," "Blue's For Duffy's Tavern," "Caledonia River" and "Gotta Be A Good'un." The other original tune from that session was "Deaf, Dumb, Crippled & Blind" which was recorded by American Blues Rocker Tinsley Ellis around 1990 or so.

In the mid '80s I was Blues rockin' with Guitar Mikey and The Real Thing when a mini-tour of Southern Ontario was arranged with The Biscuit. He was on one of his many by then familiar getting-his-shit-back-together efforts and we were like, please, please Richard, all for it, especially as he had a great new album coming out. Richard always showed up for recording sessions made available to him, prepared and straightened up and a number of great Blues records were created, many using Hamilton area musicians:

110

Jack De Keyser
John Lewis
Sonny Del Rio
Neil Nicafor

The crazy shit that went on after Richard's recording sessions and on the promotional tours is a story I've been told by several people but didn't get to experience until we were picked to do the promo tour for his then current album *Richard Newell aka King Biscuit Boy* on Stoney Plain Records. Over about a week we played a series of one-nighters around Ontario including Toronto and I did get to play again Ottawa's justifiably famous, always with great Blues audiences, The Rainbow Bistro.

After the Gooduns broke up in '74, Richard signed with Epic Records and went down to New Orleans to record with Allen Toussaint and the Meters. Special to me was that the session included George Porter Jr. on bass along with several other New Orleans session cats including Art Neville and Dr. John on guitar on one of the cuts. Of the many fabulous songs on the album they made at Sea-Saint Recording Studios, two were re-recordings of songs Rich and I had written and recorded for Paramount Records back in 1971: "Deaf, Dumb, Crippled & Blind" and "Caledonia River," adding great, new, funky N'Orlins horn and bass parts in Toussaint's arrangements. It was jaw-droppin' to have some of my New Orleans musical heroes wail on a couple of tunes I'd helped to create.

This was probably the highlight of Richard's recording career, to be in New Orleans working with the cream of the city's Funk scene. New Orleans was home to so many of the record labels and artists that Richard collected and loved. Vocally, I don't think Richard ever sounded better. And the music still speaks for itself!

Garnett Zimmerman and Richard play with Popeye for the camera.

Hot Times At The Hotel Tonight

After the Real Gooduns episode, I was supposed to be getting a job and settling down again but fuck that yeah. I got involved locally playing the Blues with Mike Oddie, harmonica and vocals, and Ronnie Copple from The Chessmen on lead guitar. I just had to play and stay abreast of the latest music trends, especially the Blues. We put a band together: Rock Bottom.

Oddie first entered my life in the early '60s, after the Caskenettes, as in Steve, the former Chessmen lead guitarist, and his brother Jimmy, moved from the central Mountain's Mohawk Gardens, out to Red Hill Valley just off Queenston Road in the city's east end. Mike lived nearby on Walter Avenue at that time and Jimmy and Mike both went to Glendale High.

One of the highlights of that neighbourhood was the new, USA-based Towers department store. They had a great, comprehensive record department where you could make surprising finds, for Canada anyway. Best of all they had this six-foot square discount table, full of just-off-various-charts-etc. American 45 rpm records. It was constantly replenished with amazing disks especially by the likes of Elmore James and Lee Dorsey on the Fire/Fury label, and more stuff from the label's owner, Bobby Robinson. Man, it was the ultimate find for The Hammer at that time. Eventually a Towers clone showed up at the plaza at Upper James and Fennell with the same sort of discount record table. All reet! Loads of stuff that caught our ears but never became big enough hits in the US to warrant release to Canada's top 40 or so, format radio, let alone sell in front-line record stores. We called these "chance" records, at 3 for $1 not much to lose. Any crap acquired this way you could always flying saucer from the Mountain brow.

Anyway, Oddie got involved with Ron Copple, who was a close friend of the Caskenettes before The Chessmen, Steve and Jimmy having delivered fish and chips by bicycle for Ron's parents' shop up on Brucedale Ave. After Richard Newell left us Hammerheads behind for the bright lights of Hogtown to become "Richie Knight" of The Mid-Knights, we needed a new front man and Blues harp player. Ron and the Caskenettes hyped Oddie as the guy to me and, to my surprise, he lived up to their promo. More than a record collector, audiophile and musicologist, Oddie really could do all the great harmonica Blues parts and sing as well. In fact, he could really belt out!

The Acetones, left to right: John Lewis, Doug Carter, Rick Hebert and Phil Cott

Ron and Mike started to hang out and worked on putting a Blues band together, listening to records, getting high and drinkin' booze and playing music. Ron didn't smoke pot but loved his cigarettes while Mike loved his pot but never smoked tobacco. In the words of Chuck Berry, "it goes to show you never can tell."

Back in those days, if you happened to own a great record there was no way to make copies for your craving friends, and extreme, home-made security checks came into force when anyone tried to "borrow" your coveted 45s or albums. To hear your hot platters friends either had to come to your place or, better, entice you to their place with the promise of a good time if you brought such and such records with you. People had different record players then, from tiny, tinny, portable dresser-top units to state of the art "audio systems" that played the music the way it was supposed to be heard, short of the real, live thing. Crank the volume way up amps to shake your bones. Oddie, from the get go, always had the latest in this electronic, mess with your heart, stun your brain, best way to play the great Rock and Blues 45s and albums, sound systems of that time. It originally started in the very early '70s, and was the same way forever after for the rest of his life. So if you'd picked up something good, you just had to play it on his equipment.

An electrician by trade right out of high school, Oddie was always on three shifts, working wherever. This meant he was only available for gigs two out of every three weeks. Hard to hold a band together when you finally get a gig playing somewhere and the front man has to work. I mean, like, his real job. But his heart was always in the right place, though he remained an electrician most of his working life. In his last days in the late 1990s he owned a very high-end audio shop in Dundas, west of Hamilton, selling mega-cost systems, $10,000 turntables with god-knows-how-expensive amps and speakers to match. Drop by and watch the Beamers, Mercedes, little Italian sports jobs from all over Southern Ontario pull up to the shop door, looking for the latest gizmo to lug home.

In my last attempt to play Blues and put a band together we had a couple of after-hours jams in his shop. Mike wanted to front a Blues band one

Elmer

TAVERN

CORNERS OF MAIN & CAROLINE

1ST FLOOR GREAT

MUSIC

By

Rock Bottom

2ND FLOOR
QUIET-ENJOYABLE
ATMOSPHERE IN OUR
FABULOUS

LOUNGE

"WHERE ALL THE ACTION IS"

Mike Oddie

more time. By then his joint was making so much money he was into collecting classic amplifiers, all the great old Fenders and Gibsons and some other brands too. It was great to pull out my '50s Kay bass and play through a vintage '50s amplifier. But the band never got off the ground. Neither of us had the time. It was early 2000's and my body just couldn't take the life anymore, much as my mind craved playing still.

Mike passed away in 2005, a largely unknown local Blues hero, great harp player and vocalist living, unfortunately, in the shadow of The Biscuit for all his musical career. Except, perhaps, where it counted most.

But back in the early '70s, Mike was one of the first guys I turned toward to stay in the life. One memorable Rock Bottom gig during this brief period was at the Park House Tavern at King Street West and Locke Street North. When we got there, our first night at this place, it was full of bikers. Turned out it was the beer hang out for the Red Devils M.C., who had a clubhouse further south on Locke. One of the former members of The Chessmen, guitarist Andy Torkelson, had become a Red Devil along with his younger brother Brian. These boys liked their Blues and even had an in-house band featuring the Torkelsons. Must have been how we got the job. During the last set most of the gang came on stage to sing, blow their harmonicas or just dance. We could hardly find room for us to play. Talk about having your cool tested. Fortunately I was experienced with such phenomena. The St. Catharine's chapter of Satan's Choice had done the same thing back when I played with the Fraser Loveman Group. Man. The things people did before karaoke.

But Rock Bottom could never find a drummer right for the music we wanted to play. Eventually, on the advice of Michael O'Brien, we checked out Pat Finochio, a local skinner who loved and could play the Blues, and through him, eventual Juno Award winning lead guitarist Jack De Keyzer, Mountain boys both. Thus the F.L. Kyng Blues Band was born. That was "F" and "L" as in "fear" and "loathing"; we were all huge Hunter Thompson fans. On some nights though, when things got uncoordinated due to whatever substance, it was "F" as in Fucking and "L" as in Loose.

We played gigs at various pubs and special events around The Hammer and eventually through Michael O'Brien sweet talking the manager, we got into the Elmar Tavern as one of the groups in their four-band monthly rotation. It suited O'Brien to have another band that was similar enough groove-wise to his own band, M&M, both bands satisfying the same fan base. At that time the Elmar was one of the hottest, hippest places to party in town.

Elmar Tavern contract, 1973

> hey!
> a regular gig!
> a chance
> to build a following
> allllll reeeeeeeeeeeeeeeeeeet!

The Elmar had three rooms. The one upstairs had a fireplace lounge with lots of easy-chairs and the first proper pints of draught in town served in ice-cold mugs. Two rooms downstairs. Up front, the north, Main Street side, was the familiar, men-only, draught room with pickled pepperoni and hard boiled eggs in big jars on the bar. They were two of the main foods for die-hard beer hall regulars who, as they bought bags of chips, seldom failed to comment on the offerings' similarity to oversized genitalia. Anyway, the big room with the bandstand and mini dance floor was at the south end of the building.

Friday nights the room would fill up early and there would soon be a line-up to get in. Friday was always the night to go out and party in the hotels and clubs around The Hammer, probably still is. In a blue collar town Friday is payday. "The eagle flies on Friday" as that old Blues standard "Stormy Monday" has it, only in Canada I guess it's the Queen that has wings. Another difference, in Canada we didn't wait for Saturday to go out and play. The Elmar would quickly fill from floor to ceiling with a combination of people and cigarette smoke. The first set was usually quiet on the dance floor as people socialized and sucked back beer, rye and ginger or rum and coke. The band would loosen too with some easy warm-up tunes before leaving the crowd with a couple of real house-rockers as set-up for things to come. By the second set the floor was ready to shake bootie, and we were ready, ready as a band can be, to help them make their back-bones slip. Ready to rock the house all night long.

Hail, hail Rock'n'Roll
hey hey, play Bo Diddley
and Johnny B. Goode
slip in a long, slow number
will ya so when we dance
my baby can fee—eel my love
Huh! What's that?
Last call?
Yeah, that's it folks, time to go home, we're callin' it a night
More
What?
Encore
Louder
ENCORE
Louder
ENCOOOOOOOOOOOOOORE!
All reet. Mr. Bossman, don't turn those house lights up yet.

It was always "Bo Diddley, Bo Diddley have you heard" until management started flickin' the lights on and off, time to clear the stage boys, and if we played on anyway they just went to the fuse box and killed the power.

what the hell

time for another toke anyway

hey! where's the After-Gig-Party?

And on Saturday night, Sundays still dry in Ontario, no gig to be in shape for tomorrow night and having already worshipped at the house of the groove until all the clubs and pubs shut at midnight, it was party all night with whoever had beer in the fridge and would take you home to it.

Come the dawn rock on rock on!

At the corner of Caroline South and Main Street West, the Elmar was easily the hottest gig in town. Let it rock, the "high" times were here. Gold from Columbia. Jamaican Red. And the best, Elephant, stick-weed from Thailand: primo buds tied with thread to a thin branch not unlike the technique used to make "devil sticks." Rumours had it O'Brien, through his Hawkins' connections, was the source and who would be so uncool as to say it wasn't so, even if it wasn't?

Oh, and black hash from somewhere in Quebec, only the local bikers knew exactly where for sure. Was this maybe the beginning of the beginning of the biker wars, the clubs moving into heavier stuff and looking to expand? Some Hammer bikers, faces we recognized as regulars in the Elmar audience, were said to have gone down to Montreal to make connections or, like Johnny Pops is said to have done before them, their bones. A couple, Richard Newell's cousin for one, came home fucked up and shot. Maybe it was worth it. Hamilton, like most blue-collar towns, loved its bad boys. The stories hung like smoke in a crowded room.

Between sets at the Elmar, audience and band members alike headed to the narrow walkway between the tavern and the apartment building next door. Dig it: a long, skinny row of folks gettin' high.

Don't bogart—what?

Sometimes, when the club was wall to wall, we'd toke right at the tables, the cigarette smoke in the place so thick who noticed? From '73 to '76 I played the Elmar off and on with both Mike Oddie and the F.L. Kyng Blues Band and with the band Michael "OB" O'Brien and Michael Short set up called the M&M Band.

Who is Michael Short? Michael Short of the M&M Band and M&M Productions, is a great rockin' Blues pianist and wit extraordinaire. As he told it, he taught his brother Marty everything he knew. Spending a couple of youthful years hangin' out and playin' music with big brother, I'm inclined to believe it. Yeah. That Marty: Martin Short. Mike, or as his side-kick at the time, Mike O'Brien used to call him, "Greek, (I never found out why but it had nothing to do with a certain sexual proclivity), always told this story about his large Catholic family and his Mom and Dad and how the whole family got together on a regular basis when he was growing up and gathered round the piano and sang Broadway show tunes together. Talk about getting off on the right foot to try and enter American show biz. Short had this buddy, Bob Ursal, a writer and when I first met him, a newspaper guy in Hawaii, but from The Hammer; Dundurn Street South up near the escarpment. Mike grew up in Westdale and they went to school together. They used to hone each other's wit with constant repartee. Awesome to listen to and to try to keep up with, mentally and vocally. Say a few words in response to their talk and they were all over you. Thick skin time. You can see Michael's creativity in his TV and movie credits as a comedy writer. He was last seen somewhere around LA. Damn good Blues and Rock'n'Roll piano player too.

Three amigos: Doug Carter, Richard Newell and Michael O'Brien

You may remember I met OB when he was hired to replace me when I made my first step up the corporate ladder at Dofasco in early 1964. If you don't, let's both blame it on my for-some-reason mixed up memory.

He followed the music and had seen The Chessmen a few times around town. At the time he was especially interested in Bobby "Blue" Bland, stuff like "Little Boy Blue," "Farther Up The Road," "Cry, Cry, Cry" and "Don't Cry No More" which I had on Duke Records, 45s I'd picked up in Buffalo. I introduced him to other Duke recording artists of the time, like Miss Lavell, Fenton Robinson, Larry Davis and of course my favourite, the man who brought us the ultimate harp version of "Sweet Home Chicago," Little Jr. Parker, he of Sun Records and "Mystery Train" and the boogie tunes "Feel So Good" and the equally potent "Feel So Bad" that Richard Newell reinterpreted as "'Biscuit's Boogie." Pretty soon I was bringing Richard out to meet O'Brien and the world turned from there. We were connected forever no matter what would happen later in our lifetimes. I played bass with OB in several bands he formed and fronted on lead vocals and rhythm guitar, right through into the late '80s.

O'Brien loved shooting pool. It was the biggest, coolest indoor sport for males back then. It was part of the lifestyle, if you had the nerve to go. Rent a table. Have a game or two. All sorts of sports lurked in pool halls depending on the neighbourhood and sometimes not. You could be surprised who'd show up where and when, top shooters and pool aficionados always knew where the hot game in town was going down.

local vs. local

touring pros vs. local hot shots

   put your money where your mouth is

   let's see what ya' got

O'Brien was tuned in

It was mostly some version of Snooker in those days, on the great big tables and all those red balls and sets of coloured ones too: black, pink, blue, green, brown, yellow, 7, 6, 5, 4, 3, 2. Now it's all American games on little tables: Eight Ball, Nine Ball, probably because you can squeeze more tables into small spaces in little hotels and taverns. Come to think, some of the first small tables around The Hammer's beer joints were coin-operated. Yeah, the classic pool halls of Hamilton. We clocked them all over town:

Ottawa Street just south of Cannon

above the Golden Rail, King just east of John

standing room only upstairs the south side of Gore Park

a one story concrete building on Fennell just east of Upper Sherman
over the furniture store, Upper Wellington north of Brucedale
(that's a cop union hall now)
a great old hall upstairs at Wentworth and King East
a shack on Walnut, east side, just north of King
(now that was kinda' scary)
in the basement of Sherwood Bowling Lanes, Upper Ottawa and Fennell
(family-style with fancy coloured table felts and balls to match)

Hey there were no video games back then so what could a guy do? I wasn't much of a shooter but I sure did love the atmosphere. OB played pool competitively until his demise in 2009 and he always knew a good groove when he heard one.

I spent a lot of quality bass time with "The Mikes," O'Brien and Short, under the M&M logo at the Elmar Tavern. OB handled vocals and Short played piano while Rick Golka on Telecaster and Steve Bannon on Les Paul, shared guitar duties. Ray "Buddy" Fennell, later replaced by Greg "The Shark" Zark, smacked drums.

Drummers were a problem back in The Hammer during the '70s. Few could or wanted to play pre-psychedelic music, i.e. Blues shuffles, when they could be Keith Moonin' it up. So when we couldn't find a local to play that consistent, heavy and funky when necessary, shuffle beat and if we couldn't get Ray Fennell to come down from Guelph, we brought skinners in from Buffalo.

Back when Hawkins, who always wanted the very best talent in his band, began living in Ontario, he ran into a similar situation and started hiring musicians out of Buffalo who had worked with and been mentored by Stan Szelest, a legendary piano player and band leader in his own right. Szelest was known to have very great expectations of the musicians he played with so the story goes that Ronnie would show up at Szelest's Buffalo gigs when he knew a player he wanted was working. One way and another between sets Hawkins hustled his target into the back of his big Bentley that Gordon Lightfoot wrote the song about then hire the young impresario on the spot, whisking him back to TO and into Hawkins' band right there and then.

Ironically, in the late '50s Szelest, about 18 at the time, had come down to Hamilton to play with locals Jerry Warren and The Tremblers. They'd been the biggest thing in Rockabilly Rock'n'Roll around the Golden Horseshoe in the late '50s, early '60s but I never got to see them as they exclusively played the bar circuit and the drinking age was 21 then and I always looked way to young even after I was legal. So shit, too bad for me. Szelest was brought into the Tremblers by bassist Rebel Paine, also from upper New York State. Both were hired by Hawkins after his original Hawks broke up in the early '60s, Levon Helm staying on drums and Fred Carter on guitar, soon joined by the very young Robbie Robertson. And wow! It was arguably the wildest version of Ronnie's Hawks ever! Stan Szelest played stints with them until 1989, so I guess he didn't much mind The Hawk poaching talent from his Buffalo bands, maybe considering it free trade. Can't ask him. He passed away in 1991.

Szelest and a drummer named Sandy Konikoff led a very successful rockin' Blues band out of Buffalo from 1961 through 1968, very concurrent with what Richard Newell, I and other members of the Chessmen were doing out of Hamilton through that same time period. Between Richard, Hawkins, Szelest and then Michael O'Brien who brought in Buffalo cats, especially drummers as needed, the connection between the Hammer and Buffalo was cast in steel. Konikoff was OB's first choice stateside to reinforce the M&M band, even if Sandy could be a little strange. He is credited with creating what has become known as the Buffalo Shuffle, a unique and energetic take on the standard fast Blues shuffle. A two handed double shuffle. Two beats on each hand and a dotted eighth note. The left hand matches the right hand. Most drummers just play a single beat on the left hand. It takes a lot of concentration and energy to truly play the double shuffle. Sandy's protégé, Tonawanda Greg "The Shark" Zark, had that groove down too!

OB also brought in John Till to replace Rick on lead guitar for a stretch. Originally from Stratford Ontario, Till had been in the Full Tilt Boogie Band that Janice Joplin put together, recording *Pearl* just before she died in October 1970. The Mikes had met John when they worked for Ronnie Hawkins' booking agency upstairs over his Coq D'Or Tavern in Toronto while Till played for the house-band version of the Hawks below. The Full Tilt Boogie Band, which also included former Mid-Knights and Hawkins alumnus, pianist Richard Bell, tried to keep it together after Janice's demise but nothing much happened and eventually John found himself back in Ontario looking for gigs. He hooked up with The Mikes, came down to The Hammer and we had the privilege of working with this amazing, enthusiastic guitar player. Till was a master of the Fender Stratocaster and was a very Zen music teacher as well. I learned much from working with him.

O'Brien's thing for finding gigs at that time was not to run around playing all over but to find a good club to play in, play tunes that would make the people dance, that he personally liked, so they would come week after week. It worked at the Elmar but it takes a perceptive club owner to give a band a chance. End of the night, though, if the cash register receipts added up in the big black, getting the next gig there was easy. Maybe it was his years in Hawkins' booking agency, but OB sure knew how to persuade club owners to give us that first chance.

The Blues got updated some in the M&M Band too. We did a fair number of recent but relatively obscure songs that didn't make the Top 40 but FM radio was becoming the king of airwaves by then. Songs like the psychedelic Country of the New Riders of the Purple Sage's "Dim Lights, Thick Smoke and Loud, Loud Music" and "White Line Fever," as well as Chicago Blues like J. B. Lenoir's "Mama, Talk to Your Daughter" and Muddy Waters' version of "Walking Blues" via Paul Butterfield. Throw in lots of Chuck Berry, including "School Days" and "Childhood Sweetheart" with some Merle Haggard as in "Last Night the Bottle Let Me Down," "Mama Said" and "Branded Man." Lots of electric Bob Dylan too. "Down In The Flood, "It Takes A Lot To Laugh, It Takes A Train To Cry" and "Lay Lady Lay." Upon request we did a mean version of Hawkins' version of Bo Diddley's "Hey, Bo Diddley," which, being The Hammer, meant we played it most every night and probably twice. It was Rock'n'Roll Hammer's favourite anthem.

OB really liked several original tunes by Steve Caskenette and Rick Golka, both former members of my first band, Son Richard and The Chessmen. He thought they had a lot of commercial potential. My favourites were Rick's "Shakedown Boogie" and Steve's "(Reserve Me A Room At) The Rocket Hotel." Steve's "Shining Through" was another great tune we came up with an arrangement for. Unfortunately Caskenette suffered from issues that eventually resulted in the loss of his talent in the local music scene. Now and then I wonder where we'd all be now if we'd been able to keep Steve with us.

Both Golka and Caskenette spent time in the Ontario Hospital, the mental institution that loomed over the city from the escarpment edge at West 5th and Fennell. A number of "crazy" people I met on The Hammer's streets and in its schools either worked there at one time or lived there for a while. If you were creative or rebellious back then and your parents and/ or authorities did not agree, it might be hello walls and maybe a straight jacket too. I'm no expert, but it looked to me like if they got you hooked on those psychiatric drugs you were fucked forever.

In the Rock Bottom/F.L. Kyng Blues bands we began by playing exclusively Blues standards, but by 1975 we were doing non-blues tunes including Bob Marley's "No Woman No Cry" and his "Talking Blues" from The Wailers' third album *Natty Dread*. Most of us had fallen in love with The Wailers' first album *Catch A Fire*. After some time in the US, Bob Marley had returned to Jamaica where he had begun recording tunes for the local Jamaican music market. The Wailers first album for the Island Record label of England, came out in 1973. Marley's tunes were so catchy they broke into the international market and were big hits in England. "Stir It Up," "Slave Driver," and maybe my all time fave of a lot of favorite Marley tunes: "Concrete Jungle." They all came from that initial album and were all written by Bob.

Six months later the second album *Burnin'* hit the market and the charts, from which Marley and Peter Tosh's "Get Up, Stand Up" became an international anthem to human rights and still is unto this day. The laid-back but insistent reggae beat seemed the perfect soundtrack for resisting oppression. Marley's "Burnin' and Lootin'," about defying the curfew and the politicians of Jamaica, was easily translatable into any Third World culture. But the standout track was Bob's "I Shot The Sherriff," quickly covered by England's Blues guitar hero, Eric Clapton, his version sweeping the planet.

In 1974 *Natty Dread* was released, the last album by The Wailer' three-man front line of Bob,

Peter and Bunny Wailer. "Lively Up Yourself" was the hit off the album but the boys in F.L. Kyng and I preferred "Talkin' Blues" and "No Woman, No Cry" both of which we incorporated into our repertoire. Sly and Robbie, the master class in Reggae rhythm sections (bass and drums), came out of The Wailers as well. And hey, the bass lines were new in Reggae.

We also played Clapton's "(Get Your Bottle of) Red Wine," Van Morrison's "Wild Nights" and the Stones "Dead Flowers" on which De Keyser handled the vocals, giving Oddie a break from singing and letting him workout on harmonica. We did another big Stones hit, "Honky Tonk Woman" as well, always a crowd favourite. And anything else that we thought would go over with the audience, that rocked out and that could be adapted to a Blues band format. All this still mixed with a healthy dose of classic Chicago style Blues. It worked out fine. During this time I was determined to keep trying to write songs and convinced the band to let me start singing one of my own compositions, "The Shorty George." Boogie on.

> Shorty George did the boogie one night
> The people all said you ain't doin' it right
> You're movin' up should be layin' back
> Hey wait a minute! We like it like that!

And who knew in 1973 that The New York Dolls were out there recording a Rock-changing album? They followed it up with a trip to London, singlehandedly starting the British Punk movement which rapidly shot off under its own momentum. Many rockers in the first Brit-Punk bands were fans of the Dolls and were inspired to start their own groups after seeing them in concert. Punk was a return to the original Rock'n'Roll, sort of a suburban Folk revival fuelled by electricity and enthusiasm for simple chords and anger at the pretensions that had distracted Rock from its rebellious origins. Did I say "anger?" More like fury, using nothin' but down strokes, all eighth notes, maybe even sixteenths if the booze and the speed etc. were kickin' in real good, where quarter and half notes had sufficed before. Yeah, it meant learning another new bass style. In Punk everything was twice as fast as what had gone before. Like Chuck Berry on speed, the Dolls channelled enough energy to cause brown-outs on the sun, consuming too much of whatever came their way: sex, horse, they'd learned their Rock'n'Roll lessons well. Jet boys.

And then along came The Talking Heads. Wash me down you psycho killers. Loved their take on one of my favourite Al Green tunes "Take Me To the River" and David Byrne wearing those big, boxy, a-la-Elvis suits. The get-up plus his highly original "dance" moves enthralled audiences everywhere. Their first widely influential tune was a track from the album *Talking Heads: 77*, "Psycho Killer" with its catchy sing-a-long bit. Many great tunes came along later like "Burnin' Down the House" with the entire album Remain In the Light becoming the essence of rockin' New Wave music.

Dave Klinko turned me on to The Clash. Rockin' anarchy. I loved the political sentiments. He bought Sandinista! the minute it was released in Canada and we both fell in love with it all. Johnny Valentine, a local vocalist who had turned me on to the New York Dolls, in particular their exceptional vocalist/front man, David "Funky, Funky But Chic" Johannsen, also initiated me into the rites of the Sex Pistols. The Sex Pistols music I got it right away. Complete anarchy on top of a great Rock'n'Roll rhythm section. Those boys really worked it out and the lyrics were pretty fuckin' vacant eh!

Locally, Frankie Venom and Teenage Head, Dave Rave and The Shakers, Mickey deSade and the Forgotten Rebels, these were The Hammer's answers to the new Punk movement screaming out of London, England via New York City and The Hammerheads hit the Canadian Punk scene hard and pretty damned early for Canucks. All that urban angst seemed made for the city's declining industrial sector. The boys were inspired to produce a lot of original material, much of which still sounds good today. Pioneers all. Head's "Teenage Beer Drinkin' Party" is practically the national anthem on summer weekends unto today.

My friend, drummer Ron Knappett, showed up at my place in late 1974 with a copy of Waylon Jennings' new album *The Ramblin' Man* under his arm. He was crazy about it and Ron was a Jazz/soul drummer from the heart. When I first met him in the late '60s Ron's idol was Buddy Rich with Louie Bellson not too far behind, but he loved the new feel of Country music. For one thing, the drums had moved up in the mix and the bass lines had evolved too. And boy, Knappett was right. I'd already noticed that Rolling Stone Magazine had given Jennings' album a decent review for a Country record and Country really wasn't the magazine's thing back then either. But this record revolutionized the music. Nashville ended up calling it "Outlaw" 'cause the boys were doin' it themselves without the help of Opryland and Nashville studios. How dare they make their own music their own way and record it like that too? But a large contingent of the Country-music-loving public dug it and so did a whole bunch of mainstream pop fans. Again, it was a rebellion against the slick sophistication of professional studios and producers, reconnecting with a rawer, more basic expression of human emotions. Yeah. If "Take This Job and Shove It" ain't a Blues sentiment I don't know what is, but in the words of Neil Young, "are you sure Hank done it this way?"

By 1976, the new Outlaw Country, and Country music in general, began taking over bars and taverns, everywhere. Outside of the American south, rockin' bands and Country fans had not had much in common in those days, especially in The Hammer, where even a 4/4 beat Country song by a bona-fide Country singer could have been viewed as suspect. The gigs for Blues and Rock'n'Roll based bands ran out at the Elmar and most other places around The Hammer as well.

> the double shuffle
> became the two-step
> one-two one-two
> one two yuck
> don't that groove suck
> especially on bass

Blues took a beating in the '70s. Things started out strong, with Albert King exploring the Funky Blues at Stax Records in Memphis, backed by their incredible house musicians, Steve Cropper, Duck Dunn, Al Jackson Jr., Booker T. Jones, Isaac Hayes. But in 1975, while planning to put aside individual projects and spend three years in a Booker T. and the M.G.'s revival, drummer/producer/song-writer Jackson was executed in his Memphis home, shot five times in the back. The case was never solved, though Jackson had been shot in the chest during a domestic dispute just months earlier. His wife, Barbara and her boyfriend were killed in a gun battle with police in 1976. It's like some of the driving force for the music declined with this tragedy. In '71, '72 and '73 Freddie King collaborated with Leon Russell, releasing "Getting' Ready," "Texas Cannonball" and "Woman Across The River," on Russell's Shelter Records. In '74 Freddie switched to RSO Records and released the very Funky Burglar featuring some cuts with Eric Clapton, before passing away in 1976. Mike Oddie and I loved this stuff. Freddie's "Going Down" and his take on Jimmy Rogers' "Walkin' By Myself" from these albums became a staple in our repertoire. Jr. Wells and Buddy Guy were also modernizing their sounds, starting with their 1973 album Play the Blues on Atlantic Records. Muddy Waters was still going strong and Muddy and a host of Chicago and Mississippi Blues guys were touring Europe every summer but were still being mostly ignored at home. Same old, same old. The exceptions were gigs like Toronto's Mariposa Festival. In 1973 Son Seals started his career there as a guitar-playing front man after several years playing drums for Albert King, releasing albums in 1973, 1976 and in 1978, one of the great live recordings by a Bluesman, *Live and Burnin'*.

But you can't keep a good sound down forever. In 1977 George Thorogood released his first album *George Thorogood and The Destroyers*, sowing seeds among teenage guys for the Blues revival of the mid '80s. J.J. Cale's *Naturally* came out in 1972 and the influence on some of us wannabe songwriters was enormous and lasted until the early '80s. Clapton took vocal lessons from J. J. Cale and in 1974 released 461 *Ocean Boulevard*. His cover of Bob Marley's "I Shot The Sherriff" swept the planets, but I think I told you that already. Meanwhile The Meters emerged out of New Orleans eventually to evolve into The Neville Brothers who, in 1989, recorded the album Yellow Moon produced by Ancaster's Daniel Lanois.

The devil only knows what was going on in the Rock world. Post Led Zeppelin Arena Rock didn't do much for my dancing' shoes. Metal, Heavy Metal, Sheet Metal I like to call it, sub-genre after sub-genre. I failed to pay much attention but I did love the endless naming of the different types of Rock styles, my eventual favourite being Death Metal. If only.

The biggest Blues killer, probably, was the diversion into Disco. The Trampps set the groove, thumping out of dance clubs in the Philly area. Atlantic Records released their self-named debut album in 1975. When it hit the charts Disco took off. My favourite cut: "Love Epidemic." Unfortunately the Disco drum beat behind the sound was soon co-opted by every pop record producer on the planet, driving everyone round a bend big as the rings of Saturn, especially after Australia's Bee Gees reinvented their career with Disco-beat based songs, six of which ended up on the soundtrack of 1977's "Saturday Night Fever." The movie, starring John Travolta of TV's "Welcome Back Kotter" was a smash hit worldwide. Suddenly everyone wanted to dance those wavey steps and dress like pimps. Fire the drummers. Buy drum machines. Big big hats. Okay, maybe centuries from now disco will be remembered as the first popularization of early digital music, releasing an explosion of synthesizer and computer based creativity, but that won't be until long after we've forgotten that their "ha, ha, ha, ha, staying' alive" jive messed with people's minds like a lobotomist's knife.

Jain Dickinson

Sometime in the '70s I decided I could only listen to so much of the wealth of new music available in all kinds of styles. Music fractured into a dozen different directions and has continued that way with crossovers and purists in each form. The record biz boomed. I began to pick and choose stuff to listen to and buy, though I've never lost my love of the black music of the '50s and early pre-Elvis Country of the Honky Tonk vein, which grew from my inherent love for RockaBilly. Those two styles always seemed to me to be played by cats like me, white guys lost in the Blues.

In 1976, with little local work for strictly Blues bands, I heard through a friend that the new owner of the venerable Park House (where I'd played a few years earlier with Rock Bottom) had renamed the old beer hall Kilroy's and was looking for a band. Specifically a "vintage" Rock'n'Roll band. I don't think the term "retro" was being used in this sort of musical context back then, and thank the R'n'R gods for that. It's enough to be "vintage" without being called "retro." I swallowed my pride regarding my age and gave Mike O'Brien a call. OB arranged the gig. We got together with former Chessmen lead guitarist Rick Golka and a newcomer we'd met through Roly Greenway, Crowbar's bass player, a woman named Jain Dickinson, on vocals and drums. OB was the lead vocalist and played rhythm guitar while Rick blew lead and sang harmony as either Phil or Don in the numerous Everly Brothers songs we covered, from "Bird Dog" to "Claudette." The audience loved "Wake Up Little Suzie." We did Buddy too. As in Holly. "Not Fade Away." "Oh Boy." "Think It Over." "Rave On." "Peggy Sue." If a' ya' only knew!

We called the band Almost Grown after the Chuck Berry song. Yeah, we played lots of Berry, lots of Sun-era Elvis and, much to my delight, lots and lots of tunes by one of my all time favourites: Hank Ballard. Jain sang "The Twist," "The Hootchy Kootchy Koo" and "Sugaree." This was pre-Brit invasion stuff, '50s oldies like Gene Vincent's "Lotta' Lovin'" and his big hit "Be-Bop-a-Lula." Jain did tasty versions of Little Richard's "Lucille" and Jimmy Reed's "You Don't Have To Go" as well as duets with Mike, like Brook Benton and Dinah Washington's "Baby, You've Got What It Takes" and many other assorted Rock'n'Roll, Blues and R&B ditties.

In fact, some of our Chuck Berry tunes were pretty awesome, "Back In the USA," "Betty Jean," "Childhood Sweetheart," complete with background vocals in imitation of the groups Chuck used when the song needed it. For example, Etta James and the Marquees on "Almost Grown" and The Ecuadors on "Childhood Sweetheart." We also did some straight-ahead Chuck rockers like "Let It Rock," "Bye Bye Johnny" and of course the ultimate Chuck rocker of all, "Carol." And then there were Chuck's Country rockers, like "Promised Land," "You Never Can Tell" and "Maybelline," where I got to do the vocal. Yeah, a lot of Chuck Berry. Did I mention that pub anthem, "Johnny B. Goode"? Who ever gets enough of "Johnny B. Goode"?

Turned out, we were one of the first Rock'n'Roll revival bands. OB did awesome Elvis and he wasn't an Elvis clone—he could just do it,
>   *sing like a RockaBilly king*
>   *the band doing the Jordanaire parts,*
>   *rocking the place with "Too Much"*

> *waiter more beer,*
> *"Mess of Blues,"*
> > *waiter more beer*
> *or send them to the dance floor with*
> *"I Was The One" and then come back*
> *with a pure Elvis rocker like his take on*
> *Excello Records favourite Arthur Gunter's*
> *"Baby Let's Play House"*
> > *come back baby I wanna play house with you*
> > *oh baby please, please, please!*

Jain was a dream to play with, a stone Rock'n'Roll fan from the get go who provided cool solid drumming as well as solid lead and backup vocals, adding a great new dimension to our versions of the old music. She came to The Hammer from Washington State via California on a North American tour of low-class joints in an all-girl topless band called The Hummingbirds. Unfortunately Jain's otherwise delectable endowments had to be well concealed in the Grown (groan), this still being Ontario after all. No naked boobs in bands allowed.

One night, on the way out of town after a Hamilton Place gig, master note-bender and Telecaster pioneer Roy Bucannan, who'd mentored Robbie Robertson in an early edition of the Hawks, dropped into Kilroy's with his crew looking for beer "to go," just a few take-aways for the road. But oh no, not in Ontari-ari-ari-o. This ain't the States, man. So they had to sit down and hoist a few instead. A number of people came by to whet their whistles after Roy's concert and they started spreadin' the word that the man himself was here and soon the "we want Roy" cry went up. The hotel was just a-buzzin'. The crowd demanded he get up and jam with the band and so he did, but he insisted that we do our own tunes and he would play along. What an awesome treat that night. It was duelling Telecasters and delirium reigned. Don't ask me what tunes we played; I was blown away like everyone else, maybe more so. After Roy did his "thang," OB finagled some carry-out pops from the bar owner promising to replace them from the beer store the next day. Without danger of thirst, Roy and his band were gone, but the audience remained hyped and just rocked for the rest of the night.

That was a special thing, but we'd been packing the place every weekend. The owner had wanted a '50s cover band and we were doin' it for him but still doin' songs we liked too! When the crowd got too big for the former "ladies and escorts" room we were working in, they built us a brand new stage in the big, former "men only" draught hall next door. At this point Rick, brilliant guitarist that he was, was often relying on lithium, the psychiatric drug of choice back then, to make it through the nights. Finally he left the band and was replaced by Stratford's John Till. After several suicide attempts, Rick died from body failure. Maybe it was the drugs. I don't know. Buchanan also died young in 1988 and Blues harpist Paul Butterfield was gone before him in 1987. Might be something in the music.

Almost Grown at Kilroys, Locke Street and King Street West, Hamilton

With John in the mix the music got updated with some current tunes like David Lindley's "Mercury Blues" and The Band's version of "Ain't That A Lot of Love." Jain began singing more leads as well as the duets with OB. We also started doing original tunes again, incorporating songs written by Ronnie Copple: "Ass In Dixie" and "Teacher's Pet." We did Rick Golka's "Here's To You," and I did my version of the tune I had co-written with Richard Newell, one that he'd recorded twice, "Caledonia River," which was a local favourite. We did the version from Richards' Toussaint-produced, Epic recording *King Biscuit Boy*. Yeah, we were definitely bending vintage Rock to our own Blues style.

Outside in the real world, vintage was getting weird. One day I was hangin' at OB's when in walks this kid with a pompadour, black slacks and a white sports coat, the whole ball of wax. Turned out OB was givin' this kid "Elvis lessons." And the kid was paying OB money. Real green. Awesome! Subway Elvis (Michael McTaggart) also showed up in OB's life about then. What a hoot he was getting lots of media attention back in '70 dressed up like Elvis, swivelling his hips and belting out Elvis tunes in the Toronto subway system.

Back at Kilroy's, Almost Grown was getting hotter. In April of 1977 we went to Thunder Sound in Toronto and recorded Copple's "(Getting' My) Ass In Dixie" and Golka's "Here's To You." In the end though, OB couldn't find a label for them. Except for Kilroy's, where King Biscuit Boy also did a couple of gigs as did Toronto Bluester Michael Pickett and his band Wooden Teeth, the Blues in The Hammer were almost dead. They were more a life-style in the late '70s than a musical form. But man it sure was great to be in a recording studio again.

After a couple of really great years the venue went belly up. Tax problems. Everyone from the owner to the waitresses, from the bartenders to the band to the guy who swept the floors probably, got audited by Canada Revenue. What started so great ended in a big screwup! *Sorry Mr. Taxman, I have no idea what went on; please don't hurt me.*

Later I heard rumours that future Hammer Punk stars Teenage Head, who went to high school just down the road at Westdale, had swung by Kilroy's in their early days for a few beers after rehearsals and to catch the band. Maybe that's Almost Grown's lasting claim to fame. There's still a good pub at the north east corner of Locke Street and King West, in which to recall old times.

As the decade wound down, 1978 through '79, I inaugurated a series of informal song-writing workshops with Jack De Keyzer, Ron Copple and John Lewis, mostly at Jack's place on Coral Drive just south-west of Upper Gage and Mohawk, where in the basement he was learning to become a full time musician. We also did a couple of song-writing sessions at Lewis' place. They both had simple, two-track, reel to reel tape recorders. Between us we also had a couple of microphones, but no drummer as that would have just got in the way. And anyway, if we needed drum sounds one of us would smack percussion on a guitar case or a vinyl chair back, Excello Records style. It was a fertile period for us and song-writing. We all used the experience to learn the craft, creating several decent though mostly unheard by the general public, original tunes. A couple of Ron Copple's ended up being performed by Michael O'Brien and one was recorded by O.B. as I mentioned earlier. John Lewis eventually wrote and recorded an album. Jack, after a tour with neo-RockaBilly legend Robert Gordon, joined the RockaBilly outfit The Bopcats and contributed several tunes to their first album. After that he was off and running and is still writing and recording to this day. A number of his albums have been nominated for Canada's Juno Awards in the Blues/Roots category, winning in 2003 for the album *Six String Lover*. He has also won several Maple Blues Awards, given out yearly by the Toronto Blues Society.

Until the writing workshops, Jack referenced George Harrison as his main influence, but talked about his interest in learning to play Blues guitar more authentically. I set him up to visit Richard Newell. For the questions Jack had about playing the music and playing it on guitar, I knew only Rich could give him the answers. I took him across the Mountain to Rich's place on East 25th and explained what was up. It worked out very well. Eventually, through Richard, Jack worked with Ronnie Hawkins' Hawks before heading out on his own to learn the band business and grow as a guitar player.

The King Biscuit Boy's career, though, spiralled in a familiar pattern. The fabulous New Orleans recording with Allan Toussaint proved to be another creative triumph and commercial dead end. The record company gave the album scant support and little appreciation. At about the same time, Jackie, his wife, left him, taking his young son, Richard Jr. At times like this Richard found consolation with a too-familiar companion, often brought to his door by friends showing up all hours of the day or night, always in exchange for something. Too often it was to rub shoulders with Richard's near success and to commiserate about a world that always conspired to keep a good ol' boy down.

I won't feign innocence here. The music world thrives on informal connections, friendships formed with acquaintances of other acquaintances sharing stories, information and exchanging skills in impromptu jam sessions. It's a life as much, maybe more, than a business and hootch has a well-earned reputation as a social lubricant and handy depressant for the inhibitions that slow connection and creativity. One way and another, weren't none of us tea-total.

Richard and Mike Oddie

But some are consumed by the Bluesman's life more fully than others. For most of us, this Blues might be called "Somebody Done Stole my Gal"; sad and all too common. Sing your song and move on. For Richard it was more like "I Believe Another Mule is Kickin' in My Stall." What must have hurt like a Robert Johnson stretched chord was that Rich's wife and kid ended up with his closest, cross-town, musical rival, Mike Oddie, the guy who started filling in locally when The Biscuit moved up and away, and reliably held his place when Richard returned with his tail down. Suddenly all of Richard's professional and personal ambitions were twisted into one, insurmountable knot of "close, but not good enough."

It wasn't Mike's fault. He'd been taken by Jackie first time he'd laid eyes on her, long before Jackie had a nose for Richard. And Mike couldn't help himself; he was hooked solid and endured his own longing until persistence finally paid off. But for Richard, it wasn't the kind of thing you get by easy. In the late '80s John LaRocca's Blues Society held a Muddy Waters' Tribute at The Gown and Gavel in Hamilton's pub-and-club-central Hess Village. I have video from that mostly festive event, including a few sad seconds in which Richard leaned into Oddie's ear and whispered "—you stole my fuckin' wife—."

And that's the Blues, man. The real, down home, pit of the stomach, shit-kickin' Blues. Like the Head said: "some kinda fun."

Doin' The Snake!

In the late '70s I'd just got into art-making when I became reacquainted with Dave Klinko who was a drummer I'd worked with back around 1969-70 in the band Messenger. It turned out we both had used the Dundas Valley School of Art in Dundas to further our knowledge and we started hanging about a bit, sharing and interacting to push ourselves to do and learn more both musically and making art. Sometime in the late '70s he'd taken winter holidays in Jamaica two years in a row, coming home with the 45s of the Top 20 on Jamaican radio. He made up cassette tapes for me. What a wonderful introduction to the world of Jamaican music, beyond what I'd known of Peter "Legalize It" Tosh and Bob Marley. I'd seen Tosh and his band at Ontario Place where he'd come floating onto the stage on a unicycle. Then holy serendipity, one day back in the late '70s, wandering the used-stuff shops of James Street North and Barton Street down past Sherman North, as was my wont every couple of weeks, I came across a treasure trove of used 45s from Jamaica.

    3 fer $1
spend what I got on me
anything that might look half decent
awesome stuff among the shit
Pre-"Catch A Fire" Wailers on Coxsone Records
written by Marley

"I'm Gonna Put It On"
"Africa" by the Mighty Diamonds on the Well Charge label
"More TV" by the Ruple Edwards All Stars
backed by "Little TV Big TV" by Unity Unlimited
sends me back the next weekend to buy another stack

Towards the end of the '50s Jamaicans got keen on Rythm'n'Blues, particularly a record released in Jamaica in 1959 called "No More Doggin' " sung by Roscoe Gordon on Vee-Jay 316 in the States. They worked with it and created their own lyrics for it and Ta-Ra: Ska! which is said to come from the Jamaican's word for the sound a guitar makes on the upstroke. From 1959 onwards this was all the rage. In 1964 Ska or Bluebeat, as it also came to be called, began a growth in popularity among white British teenagers. Think Desmond Dekker and "Israelites" and Milly Small's "My Boy Lollipop." Ska of course begat Reggae. One of the best reasons on the planet to get stoned. No wonder I was diggin' the Reg-eye so easy from the start. Remember back in Chapter 2, Roscoe had this crotch-to-crotch groove that apparently lives on. Other artists such as Johnny Ace, Floyd Dixon, Shirley & Lee, Fats Domino and T-Bone Walker have all been cited as influences in the development of post World War Two music in Jamaica. The music of downtown New Orleans was heard night and day throughout Jamaica in the '50s and '60s. No fools those dreads!

I think nearly half the records and CDs I've collected over the years came from used-goods stores and discount bins. For decades I followed the music trade papers and mags like Rolling Stone. I've always known what new music to take a chance on, based on reviews and articles, though being a musician around The Hammer meant being perpetually short of the readies. It helped that I had specialty tastes compared to the main stream and often found the kinds of music I loved had never sold well to the general public for one reason or another, ending up in those discount bins for me to find. Always, to this day, there's lots of stuff I like in the discount and especially in the trade-in stores. I guess starting my 45 Blues collection at Ross "The Square Toss" Boss' used jukebox record joint in Buffalo jump-started that ongoing process.

The Hammer already had a Jamaican community back then. Somewhere around the same time one of my friends came up with a bag of the strongest pot I had ever got high on to that date.

> *it too was Jamaican*
> *red*
> *temple weed*
> *Klinko finding island 45s on holiday*
> > *me finding island 45s on Barton*
> > *somebody putting good island weed on offer*
> *coincidence?*
> *no, no, I think it cannot be*
> *it must be fate, brother*
> *sign me up for a Rasta!*

Below: Keith Lindsay

Dave was soon talking up the idea of making our own music. I said I knew how that worked. I had some lyrics I'd been working on but I needed to interact with some other musicians to move them along closer to song form.

> *cool*
> *how?*

Electronic keyboard whiz of the first generation, Keith Lindsay, when we told him of our idea, was enthused as well.

I had stayed in touch with Keith who had also been in Messenger. We had gone out into the world around The Hammer a couple of times and done some black and white photo shoots as well as exchanging what's hot and what's not in the continually changing music scene. Keith turned me on to the electronic Herbie Hancock, who I'd heard a few times on his earlier acoustic piano, Blue Note releases, like the album Maiden Voyage, and his work with Miles etc. that Mike Oddie owned and I occasionally heard but hardly understood at that time. The later, electronic "Head Hunters," "Thrust" and "Man-Child" returned to a jazz where the R&B influence was more pronounced and I dug it straight away. Keith had an idea where we would use some of this and he had a friend, "Jimbo" James Gallard who wanted to get in on this creative opportunity too. Jimbo played amazingly funky James Brown style rhythm guitar and he had a 4-track Sony, reel-to-reel recorder he was dyin' to make maximum use of. Game on! Nothing like a little creative competition to push one's limits and expand one's sensibilities, I sez. Choose your poison and let's blow.

It turned out Keith and Jim were good friends with a trio of brothers, Norm, Larry and Harry Thorton, who had started out as roadies and sound men for Crowbar and now had their own music-equipment store in Burlington, called, conveniently, Burlington Music. They owned an old farm up in Carlisle, north of the city. We were welcome to go up there any time and jam our tunes and record. Them being in the music equipment sales and sound-systems-for-rent business, there was always used equipment laying about the farm house. Stuff that we soon made handy in our recording ambitions, especially mixing boards with which we were able to combine several microphones that were also laying around or ones we might borrow from the store.

> *brilliant*
> *we'll use that*
> *little bit of this*
> *some o' that over there*
> *pinch more o' this*
> *you got anything else?*

Right away, Dave, drummers being drummers, rounded up a bunch of microphones on his own so he could mike most of his drums, particularly the bass drum and of course the snare. We gave up one track exclusively to the lead vocal. That was an absolute necessity. The other two tracks were given to strategically placed mikes out in the room to pick up the bass amp, the guitar amp and the keyboard amp sounds.

A date was set up to go out to Carlisle and try this idea out. I got busy and pulled a few of my newest lyrics together and worked out some bass parts and basic chord changes. Keith came up with a few lyrics of his own as did Dave later on. Crude though it was, enough good things got down on tape to make us set a date for the same time the next week and we were to all go off and workshop what we had done and learned. I was inspired to come up with what I hoped were very-contemporary-for-that-time new lyrics and chord changes.

We recorded several of these gatherings over a period of months, calling them The Carlisle Sessions with Keith Lindsay on keyboards, Klinko on drums, me or Neil Nicafor on bass and Jimbo on guitar. One time Jack De Keyser played on two of my tunes, "Blues Started In Egypt" and "Answer To The Punkers." Everyone, including anyone hanging around the house were drafted to perform on percussion, background vocals, and ambient sound, as needed.

Keith and I smoked the odd joint or pipe of hash during these sessions. Jim didn't partake and Dave only sparingly. He had trouble handling the caffeine in a cup of regular coffee back then. Even the caffeine in a cup of Orange Pekoe could be trouble. God forbid one aspirin. Neil and I were the only ones with a six in our back pockets but Neil didn't toke either. Aw the memory of the good old days when you could get away with a little drinkin' and drivin' while tokin' too.

This was one of my favourite creative periods of my life. Of course nobody knew how to market what we'd done as demo's to record companies, but for a few weeks we had an underground reputation with certain musical factions within The Hammer due to passing around tapes of three of the better tunes from all the sessions: "Doin' The Snake," "Angry Middle-Aged Whiteman (I Wanna' Learn How To Dance)" and "Move To The Moon." What started out as writing conventional song forms and interpreting them, somehow in new ways, evolved over the period of these sessions until we totally cut ourselves loose from the conventional notions of good song-writing. We mixed Talking Blues vocals with Reggae and American Funk and good old rockin' Blues side by side along with all sorts of ambient sounds. We had also recorded a number of experimental instrumentals that mixed live playing with recordings that we had made out in the world, including a close-up of a train going by. Very percussive. Very industrial. I used a number of the tracks for the sound I played throughout the opening of my first visual art exhibition at Hamilton Artists Inc. on James Street North the summer of 1981. The last complete tune we did, "Move to The Moon (takes 1 & 2)" is still my favourite of all we attempted to create. Well "Doin' The Snake" is a very, very close second. Good fun and creativity had by all.

Oh! Oh!
here come the '80s!

The decade began with a stutter. Joliet Jake and Elwood Blues had begun showing up on *Saturday Night Live* skits late in the '70s. We loved the act, but more for the laughs than the vocals and Blues harp licks, though the duo was backed by some solid, experienced talent straight from the get go. 1980 and the movie hit the big screen with the impact of a 300 car pile-up. The Blues Brothers has since achieved cult status, and probably helped, uh, transition James Brown's and Aretha Franklin's careers. My favourite moment from the movie is John Lee Hooker singing "Boom Boom," with Pinetop Perkins and Big Walter Horton in Chicago's Maxwell Street market. Classic. But unfortunately, in The Hammer at least, the movie's more immediate musical influence was overshaddowed by another big screen blockbuster of the same year.

Having practically killed the Blues with disco in the '70s, John Travolta dealt a second blow with the release of *Urban Cowboy* in 1980. Suddenly everyone wants to wear cowboy hats, boots, chaps, spurs and those two-tone satin shirts with the pearl buttons. C&W goes mainstream. The Jockey Club at Barton East and Ottawa North got a mechanical bull and you couldn't get near the place for the crowds. One way and another, everyone's ridin' the bull and musically, I'm back in survival mode.

Even Rock'n'Roll revival was washed away. Drummer/vocalist Jain Dickinson picked up some gigs playing with weekend Country outfits, eventually joining the Dave Checkers Band. As so often happened, Checkers was looking for a bass player and Jain recommended me. No work in the Blues so I go Country. Black jeans, black cowboy shirt with pearl snaps and eventually a full beard just like Dave Checkers, which, like Ole Willie hisself, was C&W stylish at the time. Dave carefully explained the need for band members to fit in with the fashion expectations of the audiences in the joints we played, so it was no more of them flash Rock'n'Roll outfits. OK Dave, but I don't wear no hats. Dave was from tobacco country out around the Simcoe and Brantford areas. The black cowboy shirt quickly wore out and we split. Even a dyed in the wool country boy can only play

The Dave Checkers Band: Jain Dickinson, Trevor Eastman, Doug Carter and Dave Checkers

"Take This Job and Shove It" so many times before heeding its advice.

It was "so long" Dave but not Country. Jain picked up gigs in the same joints we'd been playing fronting her own trio; I become her regular bass player. Checkers' guitar player Trevor Eastman came with us and we played a lot of Country mixed with some oldies: Willie Nelson's "Blues Eyes Cryin' In the Rain," Patsy Cline's take on Nelson's "CRAZY." Jain always did "The Twist" the Hank Ballard way and audiences still loved it. But man we worked a lot of dives. That's where the work, if you can call it that, was. All along Barton Street East, up one side of James North and down the other.

The International House at James and Barton. Copper John's a few blocks further along, and across the tracks to the Genesee and The Picton House. Closer to downtown, the Grand which was next door to the Tivoli Theatre before being torn down (and before the Tivoli fell down). One of the crudest, nastiest beer joints around, I forget its name if it ever had one, was at Mulberry and James North. I think the cops finally closed that joint. A little further east we played The Colonial on a corner of King William at Ferguson, what was then

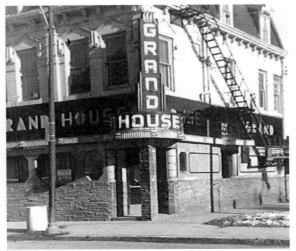

The former Grand House at Wilson and James Street North,

deep, downtown rounder country. And while we're talking "deep," deeeep in the north end, The Picton House could be very scary too with its history of tough longshoremen and neighbourhood take-no-shit violence. But the Moosehead, at Barton near Wentworth, was plain downright weird: bag-people zombies following the groove out onto the dance floor to either dance with themselves or stare unblinking at the band. Some nights you found yourself staring back, maybe on some other-than-musical level communicating with them. Do-dah do-dah, do-dah do-dah, time to get out the foil hats, beam me up Scotty.

Other edgy venues we played included Hagersville's New Alward, home of a collection of Braves who mostly hung out in the back room bitchin' about Whitey and treaties and such but were generous enough about our playing to leave us alone on the bandstand when they could have been kicking the shit out of these white Blues guys who couldn't play Country worth a damn. Jain and I even played at the hockey/lacrosse arena in the centre of Oshweken, the town on the Six Nations Reserve, with O'Brien and Ron Copple. They took to our takes on Chuck Berry, Gene Vincent, Elvis and others of that ilk, including Hank Ballard (have I mentioned one of the big

Last gig with The Breeze:, left to right: Ron Copple, Brent Dawson, unknown drummer Doug Carter and Trevor Eastman

connections between me and the other half of the rhythm section was our mutual love of Hank Ballard and the Midnighters?) and Aretha Franklin, edging a bit toward the Rock and Bluesy side of Country. Maybe, when it came to Country, it was more cowboys than Indians.

We also played a zombie joint down by the Grand River in Brantford a couple of times. I swear the place must have opened when Brant first forded the waters, somebody picking the spot to provide poor, sodden travelers with alky-haul to help them on their journeys and it appeared to have worked because they'd been doing it ever since without evidence of sinking another nickel into the day-cor. The joint survived somehow, and so did I, somehow, on about fifty bucks a night minus my bar tab.

Back in The Hammer, Brent Dawson, Ian Linton and Danny Lockwood were three musicians (vocals, bass and drums respectively) who grew up together on the Mountain. With Ron Copple they put together a rockin' weekend Country band called The Breeze. When Danny left to play full time and Ian wanted some months off to deal with other business, Copple recommended Jain, myself and Trevor to Dawson to keep the band afloat in the interim. Hello The Kenilworth House, the east-city establishment where Brent had a regular gig. Between that, the International House and an occasional party gig we stretched out our run a while longer, still too Rock and Blues oriented for most places around town however. Maybe it was our own party habits but in short order Jain and Dawson had a falling out and then Ian came back and that was that, it was back to Jain's trio format.

Takin' a break from wranglin' tunes: Jain Dickinson, John Lewis, Doug and Mike Oddie

Call us The Tunewranglers, Jain and myself augmented by an extra guitar picker or two, depending on the size of the gig. Lance Keirnan, Phil Cott, Trevor Eastman and John Lewis were among the guitarists and we'd check Rick Golka out of hospital for an evening if none of the others were available. That usually meant someone had landed another gig on a given date. Bookings were so scarce band members had to scare up their own work if they could find it. Still we managed to progress from the usual two or three night weekend gigs to doing some six nighters with a Saturday afternoon matinee at places like the Jockey Club and the Plantation up on 53 Highway just east of Upper Gage. Man that was work. Try pulling in an audience on Monday, Tuesday and Wednesday nights, especially in a blue-collar town where nobody wanted to be hung over around the heavy equipment next morning.

Below: Cowboy Doug

Mark LaForme was the local king at The Plant and most of the Country oriented tap rooms around The Hammer. He did great covers of George Jones and the latest Country hits and he could pick guitar as well. And he could rock when the opportunity arose. A lot of players I knew from around the city played with Mark, some of them unto this day. A friend of Jain's, he arranged for our one week-long gig at The Plant. Then we went back to the dives. The Jockey Club didn't work out either. Who could compete with the endless playing of Robert Palmer's "Addicted to Love" on the heavily amplified jukebox during every break, every night? Geez! I don't think our band had as much of a sound system as the juke had. I guess Palmer was flavour of the month the time we played. That's when the local tarts waiting for the steel works' shift change, would get up and dance, trying to look like the Euro-trash models on

146

heroin in the Palmer video, or something. It didn't look or sound like Country music to me. At least there was more leeway in the music choices one could play in the backstreet taverns. Baggies don't care.

The Hammer has always been a play hard, work hard kind of place but fortunately the weekend started for some on Thursday nights. It might be a freezing January Monday night cold enough to crack the water main at the bar door and sideline the mechanical bull for repairs but it was always the band's fault if no one showed up beginning of the week. Both The Jockey and The Plant were stone cold Country joints so better not play more than one or two Rockers a night. And nothing so loud as to disturb the paying patrons, or it was find another place for your noise. So you can see what a breath of fresh air it was when Jain landed that Rock'n'Roll gig at the arena on the Six Nations Reserve in downtown Oshweken and nobody threatened a hair on our heads.

But it was a cold, cold New Years Day night, like about minus 20 outside the International House at James and Barton, where I had one of the scariest nights in my C&W history. Mark and I were sitting with Jain in her blue-white classic Caddy, the one with the big fins and white leather seats, in the parking lot beside the International, passing a joint between sets. It was so fuckin' cold we couldn't imagine any sane cop would sacrifice the warmth and familiarity of Tims to be out and catch us, but all of a sudden there was some guy half in the car flashing a badge and hollering "GIVE ME THAT JOINT I'M RCMP."

Below: The International House today, Barton and James Street North

    Holy Fuck!
    We're done for
The narc's hands around my throat squeezing tighter and tighter somehow only helped to speed what was left of the evidential doob down my throat. The most he could make of it was to yell at us for a while then fuck off. Then it was back for the next set in the International, which

seemed pretty much dead-as-Marley after the scare in the parking lot. Whew! Last time I smoke a joint in a parked car. Give me open air and room to maneuver from now on.

The 1980s, for the Blues, it was definitely a case of "Are you tough enough?" Just as the Blues looked to have run out of steam across North America the Vaughn Brothers appeared out of Texas. In 1979 Jimmy, with Kim Wilson and the Fabulous Thunderbirds, released "Girls Go Wild" and in 1980 "What's The Word" but their mix of Texas and Swamp Blues styles didn't achieve national exposure until 1982's "Butt Rockin'." After playing lead guitar on David Bowie's Let's Dance album, in 1983, Jimmie's younger brother Stevie Ray, doin' his guitar 'thang' in a power trio set up, released *Texas Flood* with two great dance-floor tunes: "Love Struck" and "Pride and Joy." It's a hit and even more so 1984's "Couldn't Stand the Weather." The Blues are back in demand again as long as it fits the new demo-graph by which I mean Stevie Ray style, three-man Blues. And Ontario loosened the drinking laws, opening the way for neighbourhood bars. That meant new places to gig!

The Blues are a root music, playing a role behind every other form developed in North America, from Jazz and Rock to Tin Pan Alley, the classics and even reaching now and again into other roots' offshoots such as Country and Western. Trend or fashion might blow the

Below: Guitar Mikey and The Real Thing on the Jackson Square rooftop, King and James in Hamilton. Left to right: Mike McMillan, Doug Carter and Claude Des Roches

Blues out of the popular clubs and off the hit charts for a while, but, closely connected to the human need to express emotional pain or dance it away, the Blues never disappear entirely, always ready to rebuild audiences in a slightly altered form to appeal to the newly sophisticated ear. So when Guitar Mikey McMillan looked me up in the mid-80s and offered me the bass role in his new band The Real Thing I was good and ready.

Behind the bar at the Gown & Gavel, Guitar Mikey and The Real Thing: Doug, Robert Latzer, Mike McMillan

It wasn't our first encounter. A year before I'd answered an ad in The Spectator for a Blues bass player and Guitar Mikey had answered when I dialed the listed phone number. Mikey was heavy into Johnny Winter and ZZ Top at that moment. I said if he really wanted to learn about playing the Blues he should do what Jack De Keyser and John Lewis had done and go see King Biscuit Boy. I even gave him Richard's contact information. Apparently he did just that, playing and touring with Richard, a bass player and drummer to promote The Biscuit's latest album, 1984's *Mouth of Steel* which featured Jack De Keyser on the recording.

As always, it was a raucous educational experience. Mikey tells the story of being on the road with Richard in Edmonton. After the nights gig they were invited by a fan back to his restaurant to eat and drink half price. It was after hours and tables were put together to accommodate a dozen people down each side. When it came time to pay the bill Richard got out his share and was trying to get it passed down the table to whoever at the other end was collecting for the tab. He sat there trying to get people's attention for a couple of minutes but was ignored by everyone at his end who were loudly yakkin' and drinkin' away. Up on the table he goes on all fours and scrambles down the length of the table to deliver his money then returns the same way, latés, utensils and drinks flying everywhere. Mikey and I agreed Richard had a "badly bent" sense of humour, as The Biscuit himself had observed in one of his earlier lyrics.

But Mikey hadn't been overly impressed with Richard's business sense and the endless partying. The tour over, Mikey was planning to keep the band together and front it himself. However, the bass player was totally fried and deep into difficulties and other things from hanging out every night with Richard. Mikey had gigs and needed somebody reliable who knew the music and would not be pissed by the second set with a third still to go. He'd heard from several people that he should check me out. Well I might be just what he was looking for if he don't mind a little "smoke" now and again, mostly again.

Meantime I'd put in another year playing Country and it still wasn't doing it for me. Waltzes and two-steps had not only quickly become boring, they weren't paying many bills either. Survival mode does not afford much excitement. Thus far, moving from a McKay Road apartment in Dundas, across town to Old Guelph Road, had pretty much been the high point of my decade. And that was strictly an economy move. No, the only excitement in survival mode is maybe the excitement of staying alive.

Mikey and I agreed to meet at the International House where Crowbar 2, featuring pianist Kelly Jay, Richard and Sonny Del Rio on saxophone, had a regular gig and was playing that weekend. Top of the topic list were commitment and drinking too much on the job and eventually we got around to the style of Blues he wanted to present: POWER TRIO! Oh man, life as a Blues bass player is so much more interesting and creative in a trio. Stevie Ray Vaughn was still the hottest Blues property out there so Blues trios with flash guitarists were finding lots of work. I was so excited I hadda' be careful not to piss myself.

A rehearsal was arranged. Mikey's drummer was Claude Des Roches from the original Shakers, The Hammer's other proto-Punk band beside the Head and the Forgotten Rebels, (Claude's cousin, Dave Rave, was also in The Shakers.) Things worked out and there I was, back in the Blues. It was an awesome run straight up to 1990, playing all over Ontario, including work with some of the top Blues and roots musicians of the day.

The band was called The Real Thing. Guitar Mikey and The Real Thing. We rehearsed tirelessly for two weeks to get ready for our first gig. Of the clubs we played, about half were six-night-a-week gigs or the usual Thursday, Friday and Saturday weekends, both types often with a Saturday matinee. Occasionally we'd do a one-night stand. We played Blues all around the Golden Horseshoe and as far away as The Rainbow Bistro in Ottawa. For the first time since the Real Gooduns I was on the road again. A number of times we worked Toronto's Blues clubs including the Pine Grill, The Brunswick House, a deep skinny joint upstairs somewhere on the Danforth I wish I could remember the name of, as well as a showcase gig at the Horseshoe Tavern on trendy Queen Street West. Then, in 1988, Canadian Bluesmen Colin James and Jeff Healey released their first albums. The Blues was everywhere. Though George Thorogood had been out there since 1977 he was too basic to be a big favourite with my crowd, though his simplicity and John Lee Hooker chops and no bullshit, do-it-yourself attitude about touring and recording, endeared him to so many of the younger crowd especially young wannabe guitar playing guys. The Real Thing mostly played tunes by Johnny Winter, ZZ Top, Hendrix, Howlin' Wolf, Muddy, Buddy Guy, Johnny "Guitar" Watson and lots more.

For awhile we gigged around town and down the Niagara peninsula with a great harp player and vocalist from Buffalo, Billy Crompton. For these gigs we were able to add harp numbers by Little Walter, Jr. Wells and Sonny Boy Williamson II. Billy and Mikey played together in an exciting call and response style stretching their imaginations to out-solo each other. We made a decent recording of one night at Doc's Place up on Concession Street. Bill sounds awesome, but unfortunately was not a well man and died young.

In those days Blues guitarist Buddy Guy was the man as far as we were concerned. We were stunned when he came to The Hammer to play Gliders, a club out in the west end whose owners were into the Blues, sitting there the whole night front and centre with our jaws hangin' to the floor. The amazing Muddy Waters-like control that Buddy had over his band was incredible, bringing the volume down so low you could almost hear a waitress count her tips, then raising it up, sudden starts and stops, all with hardly visible gestures, if any. You better know the tune and arrangements playing Buddy Guy style. Total discipline. Later that

The Legendary Blues Band rocks at Gliders, Main West at Highway 2.

year the Toronto Blues Society brought Buddy and his band to the CNE. Again a wonderfully disciplined show. Again Mikey and I had to roll up our mandibles before heading home.

This was what we had to be like! From there on in we worked on the Buddy concept of playing the Blues, an enthusiasm and discipline familiar from my Chessmen days working with Richard. We'd loved running up and down the volume spectrum from a whisper to all out, full tilt boogie, making all the stops in between. Now, here it was again, after a couple of decades of go-for-it all the time volume to the max. But this was the real thing, the real way to play the Blues in a band. Muddy Waters was the primo example of this style of group Blues playing. And it suits playing in clubs. You don't need to bring stadium-rock volume to a local music-on-the-weekends pub where the audience can't even talk to friends for set-long periods without shouting their brains out. Buddy picked up Muddy's "King of the Blues" mantle when Muddy went down in 1983 and even now he still kicks ass with his continuing releases. Still the King!

Mikey came up with an idea to bring Blues "names" in from Toronto, who often were idle on Sunday nights. Like all musicians, work is work, and you can always use some extra bucks so they were coaxed to leave their beloved "Tranna" and drive down the Quick and Easy Way to The Hammer. Cats like Morgan Davis, Teddy Leonard, David Essig and Donny Walsh from Downchild. Eventually we added local Blues and Blues oriented musicians from our area as well: Jack De Keyser, Harrison Kennedy, The Biscuit, Rita Chiarelli, Mike Oddie, Naomi Taylor and some lesser known dudes who were just starting out fronting Blues bands. Front persons all. Solid Blues singers all. But also a couple of Roots Rockers: Tim Gibbons and Tom Wilson. At first we did the Sunday thing at Eddie's Tavern on King East across from Mary Street, the former Running Pump when it was the former Terminal Hotel, all this before it burnt down.

We had good enough crowds but the joint was kind of sleezy and a lot of people didn't feel comfortable sharing the space with the establishment's regular rounders, to whom the awful rooms upstairs were frequently rented. Unpainted wall board, grimy tile floors and skunky mattresses, redolent of the Blues themselves but not of the many middle-class fans we were trying to attract. Still, when they flipped us the key to one as a kind-of dressing room we didn't mind. Voila, a place to drink the booze we'd brought and partake of a toke

Cool Fool Doug (left) posing with Guitar Mikey and The Real Thing for a promo pic at The Gown & Gavel in Hess Village, Hamilton.

or two. Don't need no star on the door for that. The format really clicked after Mikey went down to Hess Village and talked the Gown and Gavel into hosting the *Sunday Night Blues Show*, upstairs in a small bar they occasionally used for live music by experimental local bands. We brought in fans we'd had at The Pump and more! Rock this house!

The Gown was a big old Victorian house. Serving alcohol on Sundays was legal in Ontario by then, but it had to stop by 11:00 p.m. Somehow this added to the intimacy and intensity of the room.

furious firing back of pints
and cigarettes
by nearly everyone in the place
good grooves
good pickin'
good singin'
good blowin'
got some good recordings
and some video tapes too!

THE
GOWN & GAVEL
24 HESS ST.S.
HAMILTON

LIVE ENTERTAINMENT

JUNE

2   GUITAR MIKEY

15-16 GUITAR MIKEY

23   HARRISON KENNEDY

30   GUITAR MIKEY

It couldn't happen today with current stay-open-til-the-wee-smalls, liquor-lounge rules and regs, not to mention anti-smoking bylaws that chase everyone out to the curb to cop a drag. I'm not saying the rules are bad, just that you need that small, 8:00-11:00 window to make a scene like that work, and everybody home to bed by midnight to rise fresh and ready for work Monday ayem.

By 1989 there was tension between Claude and Mikey. Claude had an independent income and didn't give a flying Wallenda when push came to shove, which got up Mikey's nose. I wondered at times if maybe there wasn't something more getting up people's noses then too, but who was I, a dedicated pot-head, to say? Mikey really was trying to survive on playing the Blues, and was committed to excellence in every song, every night. He couldn't handle the devil-may-care approach and Claude was quickly kaput. That left the two of us, Guitar Mikey and one Real Thing: me. Mikey hunted up a couple of other drummers for gigs, the last and most successful being Robert Latzer, but it was never the same. That's the downside of trios: one guy goes and there's not a lot left. We had more work to go around than band to get around to it.

Claude's idol had been drummer Charlie Watts and he played a lot like Watts too, which was just my cuppa Tea. We'd made a good rhythm section, but drummers with Jazz ambitions should stay away from the Blues. Maybe you remember that washroom scene from *The Commitments* movie in which the older, experienced Blues musician tells the younger kid to quit messing about, that Jazz was for wankers. It's about doing your own thing creatively while Blues means playing simpler and with the group. Precious few solos in Blues bands while Jazz cats are always making busy, busy, busy.

By this time I've got a two year old son and a long-suffering wife. We can't solve the drummer situation and Mikey is into some controversy with the main man over at the Toronto Blues Society, which means most of our Hogtown gigs have dried up. So, the pressure is on to finally get that day job, which I do, but that turns out to involve Thursday and Friday nights to 9:00 p.m. and all-day Saturday, pretty much ruling out even part-time work behind a bass guitar. Oh well. I was getting too old anyway to stay out all night, packing up at around 2:00 a.m., and then heading into work next morning with something that might be called a clear head. There was no way I could play weekend gigs. Bye-bye Blues, hello blues.

Below: Guitar Mikey and Doug at the Carnegie Gallery, Dundas

Mikey was still thinking along the lines of trying to get a major-label record deal, making a demo tape, which he did, recording somewhere around Dunnville at the home-studio of a friend.

Doug with Mike Oddie at the Carnegie Gallery, Dundas.

Unfortunately for him, this was still the era of Saskatchewan's Colin James, a cute kid with good hair and some decent chops and voice, and then it was Jeff Healy, Canada's blind Blues guitar sensation. Lordy, lordy, but can't that blind kid play? Problem was, two Blues heroes at the same time in Canada meant there was no room down at Corporate Record Company headquarters for anybody else, no matter how good or original they were. They wuz all full up.

Mikey came up with a record release deal with Jim Skarratt's Spy Records which had recently had some national success with local singer Ray Lyle and The Storm through affiliation with A&M Records. Skarratt had played with Bobby Washington's Soul Society back in the '60s, gone on to book concerts for the McMaster University Students' Union, then branched out on his own, eventually becoming proprietor of a successful club in The Hammer's Hess Village.

Because I had written a tune for the demo tape, "Blues Attack," and because of my previous song-writing experiences, most notably with Richard Newell, Mikey called me up and asked for help putting together some original tunes for the CD. I came up with some lyrics and song sketches which we worked into usable shape. Mikey also penned some good tunes and off he and his new band went to the studio. I liked the results. But -

The Indy music scene was only beginning. A wealth of small, alternative labels recording and releasing independent music was beginning to be sought out by kids and played on university radio stations all over Canada. But what did I or Mikey know about going Indy? The CD was finally released in 1990 but wasn't promoted properly and went nowhere. Mikey eventually updated his education and got a day job with a computer company writing software, moving to Chicago, continuing to play the Blues in his spare time.

Earlier, Mikey, Claude, me and OB had had a memorable night playing at an event called "A Night with You" at Capps Roadhouse, on Main Street west near Whitney in damned near Ancaster, and we'd made a great-sounding recording of it too. I realize now that it also might have been a good Indy release, but we simply did not know enough about this new way of doing business. Small, independent labels hadn't the funds to promote extensively. It was up to the bands to do it themselves. Maybe this was something more I was a bit too old for. Anywho, from Chicago, Mikey went to Clarksdale, Mississippi where he's still playin' the Blues today and putting out CDs. Me, I started making busy framing pictures on John Street North and getting more and more involved in the local alternative art scene.

I got to play one more time with The Biscuit following the release of his 1988 album *King Biscuit Boy AKA Richard Newell* on Stony Plain which needed marketing and a promo-tour of Ontario. He'd used Sonny Del Rio, Jack De Keyzer, Stan Szelest, Neil Nickafor and Greg Park on the recording session but they all had their own bands or regular gigs and didn't want to chance a road tour with The Biscuit 'cause who knew? So Richard hired the guys from The Real Thing. We played Toronto's Brunswick House for a week, then up to Ottawa and The Rainbow Bistro for another week. Richard always sobered up for his recording sessions and they were things of beauty, but putting a band together and grinding the road six nights out of seven, working in bar-room proximity to his greatest temptation, was too much for him. Once again, about a month in, the tour broke down with Richard drinking more and more every day and every night and every day and every night and forget about him after the first set and the show can't continue.

Richard's humour began to turn bitter too. He'd start a song and then after a couple of verses change the tune and the tempo on the band and then crack to the audience about what fuck ups the band was and haw! haw! haw! But on his last CD, *Urban Blues Re:Newell*, released in 1995, he wrote two songs that were perfect parodies of the life he had been leading versus the one he was supposed to lead. "Now I'm Good (Better Late Than Never)" is the story of his getting off the juice and things and walking the straight and narrow path of normal domestic life:

Might start doin' all the things I should
Then again I might not

You have to hear the tone of voice he uses on that last bit to understand. And then there's the lyrics to "Achin' Head" about waking mornings with feelings of dread. The release party for this CD was the last time I talked to Richard. I hadn't seen him in a couple of years by then but he gave me a big hug and a free copy. I've been told that a year or so after that he really did quit drinking and took care of his ailing mother, visiting her in the hospital daily.

But during the earlier tour for *AKA King Biscuit Boy* Guitar Mikey often had to take over from Richard. Good as Mikey was, audiences were there for The Biscuit, not the kid. Still, in the early days of that mini-tour, it was fun being on stage again with Richard. Sober, or relatively so, with his shit together, he could still sing great Blues and wail his harmonicas.

Here are some of my best memories of '80s gigs:

blues at Gliders (Buddy Guy, Legendary Blues Band);
opening for The Fabulous Thunderbirds at The Phoenix, McMaster University;
the Rainbow Bistro in Ottawa with King Biscuit Boy;
The Pine Grill, Toronto with Honey Boy "Blood Stains On The Wall" Edwards.

After much coaxing from Mikey, Bill Powell, organizer of Hamilton's annual Festival of Friends finally relented and let an electric Blues band play on his main stage! Lookout Folkies, here come the boogie men. Of course it was only a late afternoon gig in the band shell in Gage Park, when many devoted Blues fans might still be expected to be lifting their heads from their pillows, but it probably also meant there'd be no serious Folkies in the vicinity to bitch and moan about the amps and the volume either. So screw your hat, Jack, we cranked it up and rocked the Blues out!

Best local gig: Gore Park on a summer afternoon with Jack Pedler on drums and a monstrous sound system that scared the pigeons all the way up to Hamilton Mountain. Are we responsible for some of those old downtown buildings collapsing years later? Did we shake the foundations and loosen the mortar, starting their decline? I like to think so. A lifelong ambition fulfilled: to rock King and James.

Dave Klinko went on to be schooled at Ontario College of Art in Toronto and eventually disappeared into the Caribbean. Keith played the Holiday Inns of Ontario for a time with The Bishops' Russell Carter and eventually ended up as Harrison Kennedy's keyboardist when Harry revitalized his career working out of The Hammer back in the '80s. Neil continued his career as bassist of choice for Hamilton area Rock/Pop/Country bands and has probably gigged in every hotel and "night club" in The Hammer and Stoney Creek, one time and another. He is also the bass player in much of what Richard recorded, including *Mouth of Steel*. Jimbo continued on in his day job, Bell repair guy, and joined a Hamilton Caribbean band of many drummers, horn players and vocalists providing the rhythm guitar Funk he's so good at. Claude owned a club in Hess Village for a few years but I don't know what he's doin' now.

Poster for the Real Thing at the Gown and Gavel, Hess Street, Hamilton

COOL FOOL

If The Boogie Woogie Kills Me I Don't Mind Dyin' (All I Wanna Hear Are Those Down Home Blues)

It started when I began working at the Carnegie Gallery, Dundas, about '94, '95. I'd lived through 78s, 45s, 33 1/3s, 8-track, cassettes, each time collecting samples of my favourite music, usually second-hand bargains on sale as technology danced it's latest twist to whatever was more convenient and would send music lovers into stores to replace their cherished hits with something that played on the latest gizmos. This time I was determined to resist. I would not buy CDs. Not being a Rock'n'Roll road warrior any longer meant I could marshal my resources and wage rage against the machinations of the recording corporations who had so long conspired to squelch my ambitions. And I could do it from my family room, using their own greed as a weapon against them. A couple more tokes, I might have mailed out declarations of war. Maybe I did and forgot.

Then I walked into the Bucks For Bargains store down the street from the Carnegie. I was a gonner. There, for only 4.99 each was a whole rack of Blues CDs, including a raft of my favourite Chicago guys and a bunch of great stuff originally on the King and Federal labels. Hooked, I bought them all and soon realized a lot of that great black music from America's past was being re-released on CDs. Stuff unavailable for decades was coming out of

Poster for Bustin' Out Blues Fest, Port Dover, Ontario, 1992

western Europe, especially Britain where they had a real affinity for authentic black music from the USA. A little later I discovered that the Rhino label in the US was re-covering and re-releasing awesome historical sessions of American music from the '50s and '60s that had been ignored by the mainstream.

Around that same time, through listening to alternative radio out of Ontario universities like McMaster in The Hammer (CFMU 93.3 FM,) the Hogtown U of T's CIUT 89.5 FM and also out of TO the ethnic and the mixed programming at Ryerson's CKLN 88.1 FM. I got to hear some great new music from various parts of the planet, most notably, the London (UK) underground scene of that time. At a record store that existed just west of the Regal Tavern at Bay and King West I was able to come up with two anthologies on Ninja Records, awesome mishmashes of music styles from the past with a hip, in the know, recording mix and always with the Funk bottom makin' you wanna dance.

Hit me!

The best make-your-knees-wiggle tune of the time was 1992's "Plastic Dreams" by Netherlands dj JayDee, a longish cut of Hammond organ-inspired dance music in the style known as House.

Back in the mid-80s I'd listened to Toronto's CKLN 88.1 FM to catch the Saturday afternoon show "Sounds of Africa" which featured recordings of the continent's west coast from the likes of King Sunny Ade, Fela (who had been banished by the Nigerian government and was living in France because of the many political critiques via his chart-topping melodies) and many of their peers and mentors from several West African countries. It was also around the mid-80s that I found the weekend Blues shows on the University of Buffalo's WBFO 88.7 FM, which became and is still, now in the late double-oughts, the place to hear new Blues from America, where the Blues is now, finally, accorded the status of an original American song form, alongside its offspring: Jazz.

In 1991 Buddy Guy was "rediscovered" by the Brits. Who else? Eric Clapton invited him to appear at an all-star Blues performance at Royal Albert Hall, which led to him signing with Silvertone Records. Together they created Damn Right I Got The Blues, in which people Buddy'd inspired through the Rock era dropped in to play on the title track. And Mark Knopfler, Eric Clapton and Jeff Beck are on the play list for "Mustang Sally." Whew! And we had recently caught him at his feral best at Gliders in The Hammer and the Toronto CNE. Everything we'd seen, loved, tried to imitate and more is on that disk. He won the Grammy for the best Blues recording and went on to win four more into 2005 when he was inducted into the Rock and Roll Hall of Fame. And if you don't believe the Rock'n'Roll part check out his up-tempo, late '50s Chess recordings back when he was just 21.

But pop music by this time had lost me. After the grunge of the '80s and its depressing grooves representing whatever drugs the latest generation of kids was into, the new categories of hip-hop/rap/gangsta/etc. and their drugs of choice and whatever was going on in the "white" musical world just could not get these old wobbly knees into sync. The "new" Rhythm'n'Blues seemed to have sunk into some sort of post-Disco funk, and by "funk" I now mean "depression."

All right. It's me, I know, and not so much the music. After a while the music you first loved because it was simple and direct begins to take on baggage, influences and inspirations, new twists and permutations that you want to learn and follow, see how they play out in different contexts and in different cultures. You can't truly appreciate the fact that it was the Brits who brought this American black musical form into the pop limelight and not want to understand what they did with it, and then what was done with that. Music is a dialogue, after all.

Or maybe I was, and still am, rebelling against white pop and its marketing machine, the tendency to want to smooth things out to avoid offending anyone and so often dumbing things down in the process. I still can't think of white pop without imagining Nancy Reagan. While the Blues and Blues-inspired music urged you to get out and "shake your money maker," white pop always seemed inclined to "just say 'no'."

Say no? How simplistic can self-delusion get? When it comes to transcendence, music and drugs have always been co-dependent, and people have always sought transcendence, from love gone wrong, from lack of money, from lack of respect, from boredom, from the Monday-to-Friday, work-a-day world, and when the drug of choice is repressed, some other weird stuff always pops up in its place. Of course Metal sails along regardless, go Ozzie! but then along comes Korn and the like, who cares, same old same old, just different mood enhancing combinations.

No fool like an old fool, unless it's a cool fool.

After leaving the Real Thing and getting another "real" job that involved working Friday nights and Saturdays, I figured my playin' days were over. Figured that in my head, but not my heart. One day I got a call from guitar player John LaRocca who I'd gotten to know back in the mid-80s when he was the man responsible for creating the Hamilton Blues Society and had brought some great music to town. He needed a Blues bass player to complete his new band. Ho, feet don't fail me now. I couldn't resist giving it one more go, so around 1992 I found myself playing for The Stingrays which featured LaRocca on guitar, Willie Leigh on vocals and Blues harp and, I could hardly wait, another opportunity to play with my favourite Blues drummer, a blast from my Chessmen and Gooduns past, John "Babe" Myles.

Willie had come out of London, Ontario where he had sung and played harp for The Fabulous Sheiks. Now he was living in The Hammer where, natch, he was a professor of chemistry at McMaster U. Don't know if it was the working climate or the chemicals themselves, but he too had a craving to play in a working Blues band again.

John LaRocca is a local lad who grew up in the Sicilian neighbourhood west of James North and Barton. Like many cities, Hamilton has a large Italian community and many settled and still lived in the north end at that time. I was told his father fixed juke boxes for a living. Coin-operated businesses with their cash flows in hard currency, have at times been favoured by immigrant communities. The upshot was that John grew up in a house full of 45s. He saved the Blues that rocked and turned himself into a lifetime Blues collector and a masterful Blues guitarist. I first met him through Guitar Mikey. John was starting up a Blues Society for Hamilton. Sell memberships, then sell the members Blues concerts by known American Blues artists. He was looking for volunteers to get it off the ground.

Poster boosting The Stingrays' appearance at La Luna, King Street West, Hamilton

Some great nights went down. Summer nights the events were held at the Leander Boat Club. What a venue for dancin' the Blues. All that wood pannelling. More recently it's been used for the annual *Blues With a Feeling* fundraiser and King Biscuit Boy memorial concert. Other times Blues Society events were held at some Victorian upstairs theatre and dancehall. A raised stage with big, probably burgundy, curtains at the far end of a big wood-floored room. Long and narrow and up a long flight of old wood stairs, across from the Eaton Centre on James Street North. Featured talent included:

Albert Collins
Mel Brown
Sonny Rhodes
Snooky Prior
and
as the saying goes
many more

I got involved and soon provided an image for the fundraising T-shirts we had screened. John even put together a hard copy newsletter to distribute at events. Over a couple of years things went OK. Events were well attended. Memorable nights included a tribute to Muddy

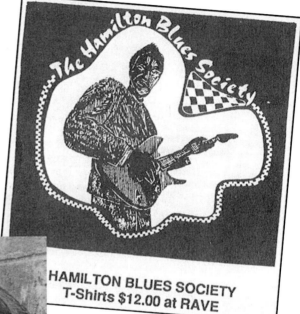

HAMILTON BLUES SOCIETY
T-Shirts $12.00 at RAVE

Above: Blues Society T-Shirt, image designed by Doug Carter.

Left: The Stingrays from left to right, Doug Carter, Willie Leigh, John LaRocca, Babe Myles.

Blues Society tickets for 1986 Halloween dance party.

Waters at the Gown and Gavel and a Blues Festival at the Leander.

I'd maintained contact with John through sharing our mutual interest in Blues and early Rock'n'Roll/JumpBlues/New Orleans R&B. *Oh man, do you really have...can I borrow it, make a copy? I just got a computer with a CD burner man.* So when he put a band together, The Stingrays, and needed a bass, who's he gonna call?

We were basically a Blues cover band. Those guys didn't write and play their own tunes, but who cared?

Blues-a-matic

John made it work for me and no gig was more than 30 minutes away from where I worked in the core, so when I got off work at 9:00 p.m. I could make it to the club for a 9:30 start. We opened for Albert Collins in a Blues Society gig at the Leander and oh, what a night it was with The Iceman. We played other joints around town for a couple of years, mostly at the Gaslight which, under the old Royal Connaught Hotel, was the main Blues club downtown in The Hammer at that time.

Well, it seemed to have another function as well. Who really knew what was going on in the "special" room out back, admittance by invitation only, other than the downtown's young Wiseguys who would drop by regular and disappear into it, along with others of the Chosen. Toot-toot-toot-tootsie, my my!

Other "hot" spots included some restaurant/bar at Young and John Street South, Mr. Laffs on

Upper Wellington and occasionally up in a strip plaza at Stone Church and Upper Paradise, all run by great guys who liked the Blues probably as much as we loved playing them, but that enthusiasm didn't necessarily translate into audiences in front of the stage Saturday nights. Most times we were lucky if twenty people went through the joint during a gig, but we still had to play three, 45-minute sets no matter what.

Above: The Stingrays on the cover of Scene Entertainment Guide, cover photo by Patti Stirling

Right: The Stingrays play The Blues Picnic, Leander Boat Club, Hamilton, Ontario.

Overleaf: Doug and Ron Copple at the First Annual Blues With A Feeling Tribute.

168

boring
boring
boring
and still more
boring
yet

and shitty money
emphasizing the obvious

When I got another new day job running the Carnegie, a non-profit art gallery in Dundas, there went my weekend gigs again.

> *sorry*
> *can't come out to play*
> *gotta go to work*

And interest waned in the Blues Society too and John closed it down. It became apparent the effort wasn't worth the non-monetary pay-back. As ever, the music moved on. Or people just got older and started to stay close to home.

In the late '90s I made another effort to get back into the performance groove one more time. But the physical work the gallery job entailed was enough on my old body and suddenly my heart knew what my head had realized much earlier: my playin' days were over. No more dancin' and playin' the Blues into the wee smalls, but I've had a good run of fun even if I don't get to blow no more!

I didn't play live in front of an audience again until the sudden passing of Richard Newell. On

169

The Stingrays' John LaRocca and Willie Leigh joining Doug Carter, Babe Myles and Ron Copple from The Chessmen at the First Annual Blues With A Feeling Tribute honouring the music of Richard Newell.

January 5, 2003 King Biscuit Boy was dead. Everything I have to say about The Biscuit I've already said. There's nothing to add here, except that later that year, when a tribute concert was put together to honour his music and his memory, three of us from the original Chessmen—myself, Ron Copple and Babe Myles—teamed up with Willie Leigh and John LaRocca to play a selection of tunes Richard had been known for and that went back to our early days starting out on East 25th Street.

It was a huge crowd

They dug it!

And that was that.

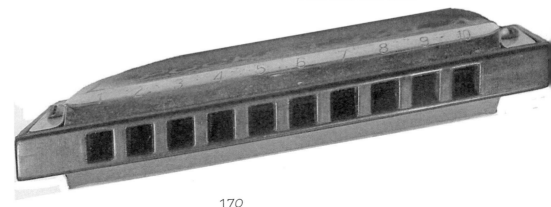